# TRIALS AND TRIBUNAL-ATIONS

## THE BEST OF THE WORST OF THE TRIBUNALS

Joe Taylor
with
Malcolm Douglas

NEW
ISLAND

Trials and Tribunalations
First published 2005
by New Island
2 Brookside
Dundrum Road
Dublin 14
www.newisland.ie

ISBN 1 904301 93 2

British Library Cataloguing in Publication Data. A CIP catalogue
record for this book is available from the British Library.

Typeset by New Island
Cover image: Charlie Haughey modelled in porcelain
by Stephen Dee.
www.stephendee.com
Printed in the UK by Cox & Wyman

10  9  8  7  6  5  4  3  2  1

# CONTENTS

*This book is dedicated to the memory of*
*James Gogarty*

# ACKNOWLEDGMENTS

We wish to thank Vincent Browne and the production team on the *Tonight* show for making it all possible. Noel Pearson for the initial impetus. Justice McCracken for sowing the original seed. Justice Feargus Flood for coming to see us twice and paying for his ticket. Susie Kennedy for looking so gorgeous in a red frock and changing for the second half. Gaby Smyth for tinkling the ivories and twinkling. Frank Mulcahy at I.S.M.E. for the first gig. Margaret Byrne for the legal advice. Kate Thompson for the editorial input. Pat Creed of Warner Music and Maurice Linnane for putting us on DVD, VHS and CD. Honor Heffernan and John Dunne for giving us a leg up occasionally. Oh, and Doyle's Court Reporters.

And finally Edwin Higel, Joe Hoban, Fidelma Slattery and Deirdre Nolan at New Island for taking us on.

# fOREWORD

## 9eNeSiS of a bOOK

When Vincent Browne approached Justice
McCracken with a view to getting per-
mission to record the day's proceedings at
the Tribunal in Dublin Castle for *Tonight
with Vincent Browne* on RTÉ, it was
deemed inappropriate. However the Justice
himself suggested that there was nothing to
stop Vincent employing actors to read the
transcripts at the end of the day. Thank
you, Justice McCracken, for creating a new
employment opportunity for thespians.

Joe Taylor and Malcolm Douglas have
been reading from the daily transcripts of
the Tribunal proceedings on *Tonight with
Vincent Browne* on RTÉ radio since early
1999. Their work is regularly included on
*Playback*, the programme that replays the

week's radio highlights. Spin-offs include DVDs, videos and CD recordings of a show devised by Joe and Malcolm which has toured Ireland from Cork to Donegal and has been described by the *International Herald Tribune* as 'a night of riveting entertainment'. The journalist from the *Herald Tribune* who reviewed the show also expressed the opinion that if such an exposé of corruption appeared on stage in New York the actors could find themselves in need of police protection.

On one memorable occasion Justice Flood himself showed up at a late night performance during the Wexford Opera Festival. He was not the recipient of a brown envelope for his troubles that night, unlike Mr Justice Barrington of the Supreme Court who on a previous occasion was given one of the dreaded envelopes during the course of a show by Joe acting in the persona of C.J. Haughey. Revenue Inspectors can relax, by the way – the envelopes contained only Monopoly money and Lottery scratchcards, which are tax exempt. Would-be bribers please note.

This book is the latest progeny of the Tribunals. It offers an opportunity to sit down at your leisure, dip in to the madness that has reigned in Dublin Castle over the last six years and savour the gobbledygook that grown men come out with when they are under pressure.

Both you and I, dear reader, know that we are not idiots. Yet that's how we were treated by our rulers and captains of industry back in the eighties when they were spending as if there was no tomorrow and the rest of us were tightening our belts. And it's up to us to make sure that nothing quite so grotesque, unprecedented, bizarre and unbelievable ever happens again.

# INTRODUCTION

Picture this: Orlando, Florida, February 1992. It is eight a.m. on a bright sunny morning and a man is going berserk. Six-foot-two with a perma-tan, the man is stripped to his boxer shorts and sweating like a pig. He is the director of a chain of retail stores that prides itself as Ireland's largest purveyor of underwear. Swinging a piece of wood over his head like a crazed King Kong, the man is shouting, 'Leave me alone, leave me alone.' He's on the seventeenth floor balcony of a five star hotel, out of his skull on a cocktail of cocaine and alcohol. It's a long way down to the white piano below him in the hotel lobby. Bono, lead singer of the rock band U2, is standing next to the instrument and hears the commotion. He looks up and sees the guy freaking out. Set against the hotel's themed décor of a tropical rain forest complete with live parrots, it could not look more surreal. A real life rock video playing without a soundtrack before Bono's eyes; it's an eerie and ugly scene. Hoping the guy will be OK, Bono then heads off for band rehearsals at a stadium 20 miles away where U2 will perform the first date of their US tour that Saturday night. Ironically, hotel staff think it's the rock band that are cutting loose on the seventeenth floor, where U2 had taken luxury suites.

In suite 1708 call-girl Denise Wojcik of Escorts in a Flash hears police sirens approaching as three cop cars respond to the emergency call at the hotel. Denise, who had been snorting coke all night long with the guy now going berserk on the balcony, wonders if the three hundred bucks he paid her for her services was worth the hassle that's sure to follow. Denise would certainly think twice before playing 'floozie in the jacuzzi' with a cokehead again. The cops confront the big guy in the boxers, who is now totally paranoid, looking like he could jump from the balcony and take some of them with him. Eventually Deputy Sam Spanich gets the big guy to calm down sufficiently for the cops to cuff him. It took five of

Florida's finest to hog-tie him and take him to a hospital. There he went ballistic when approached by an orderly wearing rubber gloves.

The cops searched suite 1708 and found over an ounce of high grade cocaine, several thousand U.S. dollars and four grand in Irish pounds. They were convinced they had busted a major drug dealer. Unfortunately for the prosecution, the search and entry were deemed illegal as the cops didn't get a proper warrant. Charges for trafficking in drugs were dropped and a guilty plea for possession of a small amount of cocaine for personal use was accepted. A fine of $5,000 was imposed and the big guy agreed to go into rehab for 28 days.

The disgraced tycoon returned to Ireland and – acting on good P.R. advice – got his spoke in first with the press by beating his breast in public and reciting 'mea culpa, mea culpa, mea maxima culpa'. It worked. Ireland forgave its prodigal son: after all, the poor guy had suffered the trauma of being kidnapped in 1981 during the height of the Northern Troubles. His own family, however, were not so easily appeased. They organised a heave and the 'man on the balcony' was deposed. He lost his job as chief executive and chairman of the family firm – a company with an annual turnover of £850 million. Little did anyone know that that bizarre news story featuring Ben Dunne of Dunnes Stores would result in the new multi-million pound industry that the Tribunals have become today.

Subsequent internal enquiries within the Dunnes Stores empire threw up a number of irregular payments. Michael Lowry, a Fine Gael Minister – whose refrigeration company, Streamline Enterprises, did business with the retailer – had his 'des res' in Holycross near Thurles nicely refurbished courtesy of big-hearted Ben. Former Taoiseach Charles Haughey revamped his wardrobe and dined out in Michelin-starred restaurants thanks to benevolent Ben's deep pockets (no Dunnes Stores own-brand cuisine for champagne Charlie). Ben Dunne may have had a hard nose for business, but when it came to choosing his friends he blew it.

In February 1997 – exactly five years after Ben's fall from grace in Florida – John Bruton, who was then Taoiseach, established the McCracken Tribunal to look into payments from Ben Dunne to various politicians. In August of the same year Justice McCracken delivered his report. Michael Lowry's 'business relationship' with Dunne was described as 'unhealthy', and a complicated web of payments from

Dunne to Charles Haughey (amounting to between £1.1 and £1.4 million) was unearthed. It was at this point that Haughey's accountant, Mr Des Traynor, came to light. Traynor had been a partner in the Haughey Boland firm of accountants. He was a tough, ruthless man with a driving ambition to make money. Haughey handed over all his financial dealings to Traynor, and short of giving him power of attorney, Haughey was content to let Traynor negotiate loans on his behalf without consulting him. Haughey had not held a bank account in his own name since 1961, so all transactions were kept at arm's length from him – an arrangement that suited him perfectly.

Traynor was a board member of the Guinness and Mahon Bank. (Coincidentally Jennifer Guinness, wife of merchant banker Jonathan Guinness, had also been kidnapped like Big Ben Dunne and released unharmed during the Northern Troubles). In 1969, Des Traynor set up the Guinness and Mahon Cayman Trust. In 1976 he was appointed Deputy Chairman of Guinness and Mahon, which made him Chief Executive of the bank in Dublin. Traynor was also Chairman of one of the country's largest public companies, Cement Roadstone Holdings (CRH). It was from the offices of CRH that Traynor set up his private, clandestine banking link to the Ansbacher connection in the Cayman Islands. In the first week of the public sitting of the Tribunal, Justice Michael Moriarty confirmed that he had almost £500,000 worth of shares invested in CRH. Justice Moriarty had not made an effort to conceal this and indeed had informed the Government about any such conflict of interest before he was appointed Sole Member and Chairman of the Tribunal. The press and various members of Dáil Éireann went to town on this. The Tribunal had not yet got up a head of steam and already efforts were being made to derail it.

Bertie Ahern said in his statement on McCracken's report: 'Honesty and truthfulness and integrity are fundamental requirements of those who serve in public life and who hold positions of great trust. All of us are deeply dismayed at the way in which in certain instances investigated by the Tribunal there has been a falling so far short of these ideals in an indefensible and disgraceful manner.'

This made the way clear for the setting up of the Moriarty Tribunal at the end of September 1997 to look into any payments and benefits accruing to Charles Haughey and Michael Lowry, particularly in relation to the Ansbacher accounts. A subsequent investigation instigated by Tánaiste Mary Harney established 120 names and funds of hundreds of millions of pounds connected with these accounts. Due to various legal obstructions the names of these account holders were not released to the public until June 2002 on foot of a High Court Order. Having sat for almost eight years, much of it in private session, Moriarty has yet to issue a report of his findings.

On 31 March 1996 the journalist Frank Connolly wrote an article in the *Sunday Business Post* claiming that a person had contacted Donnelly Neary Donnelly Solicitors in Newry to say that he had personally paid a politician £40,000 in return for a promise to have 1,000 acres of land re-zoned for housing. The headline in the paper ran 'Fianna Fáil Politician Paid Off by Developer'.

One of the greatest whistleblowers the state has known, the then eighty-one-year-old James Gogarty, company director with Joseph Murphy Structural Engineers (J.M.S.E.), had opened a can of worms which resulted in the setting up of the Flood Tribunal on 4 November 1997. (See Appendix III for a rundown of events leading to the setting up of this tribunal.)

Due to his advanced years, Gogarty's evidence was taken at the Tribunal's inception. He was in the witness box for over forty days. One of his most famous pieces of evidence concerned a trip to the house of the aforementioned then Minister for Justice Ray Burke to deliver a payment. The exact figure has been disputed (definitely £30,000 but possibly as much as £80,000). However, there was no disputing the exchange that took place in the interior of the dark grey Mercedes that transported Gogarty to Mr Burke's house, for it was well etched into Mr Gogarty's memory. His travelling companions were Michael Bailey of Bovale Developments and – Gogarty alleged but which is denied – Joe Murphy Jnr of the aforementioned J.M.S.E. An uncharacteristically ingenuous Gogarty asked, 'Will we get a receipt for this?' Upon which Bailey famously replied, 'Will we fuck!'

The Flood Tribunal became the Mahon Tribunal after the retirement of Mr Justice Flood in 2004.

Between them, the Tribunals have thrown up a whole cast of shady characters and assorted rogues:

Assistant City Manager, George Redmond, seemed to have an unhealthy fondness for money and not just his own either. The joke in Dublin Corporation at the time of George's reign was that whenever a work crew was sent out with drills to dig up a road it was really to search for a shilling that George had lost.

Fianna Fáil T.D. Liam Lawlor was more Midas than miser and liked to turn every proposition into a golden opportunity. Lippy Liam (like Michael Lowry, another refrigeration expert) was such a past master of schemes and scams that he even persuaded an ordinary Joe to wield a credit card on his behalf.

Jolly Jim Kennedy, king of the one-armed bandits, is an amusement arcade owner and Lawlor's great mate. Jim developed a virulent aversion to the media following his exposure by a persistent Charlie Bird, who wanted to know about Jim's involvement with a multi-million-pound land deal at Jackson's Way. Jim went to ground and is now firmly ensconced under the third rock to the left in the Isle of Man. It's unlikely we'll ever hear the real story behind the unholy trinity of Lawlor, Redmond and Kennedy.

And let's not forget that other reluctant whistleblower, Frank Dunlop. Ill-fated Frank broke under cross-examination and fingered a litany of county councillors who were not averse to having their palms crossed with silver.

And finally, ex-pat Tom Gilmartin, who returned to Ireland on his shining charger to reveal just how much resistance there was to new blood entering the veins of a junky economy bloated on the rampant nepotism and opportunism rife in the Hibernia of the eighties.

But, hey – why not allow the 'characters' to speak for themselves?

# AS CHARLIE HIMSELF MIGHT HAVE PUT IT ...

'It was the best of times; it was the worst of times. Bertie and the boys were back in power, P. Flynn had three houses to run, Ray Burke was in charge of passports and Liam Lawlor was Chairman of the Ethics Committee. I couldn't have planned it better myself. Then, disaster. My pal Ben got nabbed in Florida for doing a line or two with a slapper in a bathtub. I wasn't the only Charlie that Ben blew his money on, but before you could say GUBU they were on my case. Meanwhile, some Blueshirt offered a reward for any information about corruption in the planning process. It was an offer that nearly bankrupted the State when one witness came forward. The

'Planning' Tribunal was set up and the meter started ticking as the lawyers' fees clocked up quicker than a Lottery roll-over. Even I could not escape from the practitioners of the Black Arts and have had to suffer the ignominy of hustling for money to pay my legal costs. I'm a great admirer of John Rusnack, the man whose very name sends a cold shiver of dread through the shareholders in Allied Irish Banks. John Rusnack: the banker who treated his employer's funds as if they were his own. I did the same with the leader's allowance when I was Taoiseach. Indeed, every Fianna Fáil Cumann should have a portrait of John Rusnack as an inspiration to its members to think big. Because if you get caught you will certainly look better in the dock wearing a Charvet shirt than a drip-dry nylon one from Dunnes Stores. Rusnack is the only man who took more money out of Allied Irish Banks than myself and Garrett Fitzgerald put together. But unlike me, Fitzgerald and Rusnack lost all the money again, gambling on the stock exchange. Some people just don't know how to be a good time Charlie.'

1

# COLLECTIVE AMNESIA

The Flood/Mahon and Moriarty Tribunals – love them or hate them, they just won't go away, as a lot of people would like them to. Although, with a proposed drop in lawyers' fees on the cards, the Tribunals' shelf life will be severely curtailed and probably won't last for as long as the dinosaurs.

But since you and I – the public – are going to have to foot the bill, we might as well get some enjoyment out of them, even though the Taxing Master James Flynn has declared that they are 'Frankensteins spiralling out of control'.

And what's the evidence for that? Well, let's take a look at the monster the Flood Tribunal has become:

- The Flood Tribunal (or Mahon as it is now known) is in its eighth year of sitting.

- It has spanned two centuries – indeed, two millennia.

- It has been abandoned twice because of bomb scares and once because a senior counsel – who shall remain nameless – was smoking in the toilet and set off the fire alarm.

- One of its principal witnesses was arrested at the airport on his way back from the Isle of Man with a bag of swag. This resulted in a bitter row between the Tribunal team and the Criminal Assets Bureau who, according to Justice Flood, 'wanted to pick only the red apples'.

- Another witness, a member of Dáil Éireann no less, has been in and out of jail like an old lag for failing to cooperate with the Tribunal.

- An ex-Minister for Justice has also gone to jail (where he was a model prisoner who got full remission for good behaviour).

- Another ex-Minister has settled up with the Revenue Commissioners.

- There have been referrals to the High Court and the Supreme Court and a trip to Guernsey in the Channel Islands with bucket and spade to dig up more dirt.

- A number of the lawyers have left to take up private practice as they felt that they could earn more in that sector – even though eight of them have become millionaires from Tribunal fees.

- A number of the witnesses have taken up acting as lawyers and have developed their own unique brand of cross-examination, which at best is akin to a game of charades and at worst could be described as 'meandering'.

- The Sole Member of the Flood Tribunal has been replaced by an heir and two spares: Mr Justice Alan Mahon, Mr Justice

Gerald Keyes and Ms Justice Mary Faherty.

- The terms of reference for the Tribunal seem to have been based on determining the precise length of a non-existent piece of string.

The Tribunals gave rise to one of the most amazing outbreaks of collective and selective amnesia ever seen by modern science. People from all walks of life, with absolutely nothing in common except a penchant for not playing by the rules, when asked to give evidence to the Tribunal suddenly can't remember simple facts like meetings they had, who they met, important dates and large amounts of money that went through bank accounts which they never knew existed.

The Alzheimer's Society should really get special funding from the Government to carry out case studies on the Tribunal witnesses to see if there is a pattern. Such as: the deeper the shit you are in, the less you can remember.

Ben Dunne, former managing director of Dunnes Stores, was questioned about a meeting with the Revenue Commissioners which saved him almost £23 million on a tax bill. Ben had no recollection of the meeting. He said he must have suffered 'a mental blackout'. He told the Moriarty Tribunal: 'I have a good memory for figures and I am at a complete loss. If you negotiate something down from £38 million to £16 million … I find it incredible that I cannot recall, but the truth is, I cannot.'

Lost in there in Ben's brain with all the other multi-million pound savings that make up a dull day in a shopkeeper's life.

Mr John Byrne is a property developer. His key companies are Carlisle Trust and Dublin City Estates. John Byrne is the man responsible for the concrete monstrosity called O'Connell Bridge House. It used to be known as the old Harp building but it now advertises Heineken. Either way it's still taking the piss out of the taxpayer as it earns Mr Byrne millions of pounds a year, all paid by the State which rents the building for Government offices.

Mr Byrne was questioned by John Coughlan, Senior Counsel for the Moriarty Tribunal, about his dealings with Des Traynor. Traynor had been a director in Byrne's key companies for thirty years and had set up the Ansbacher accounts in the Cayman Islands where, surprise, surprise, Byrne's property empire is reported to have its headquarters. Traynor was often referred to as 'Haughey's bag man'.

Coughlan: How many other
times did you give Mr Traynor

£50,000 or a similarly large
sum for fees?

Byrne: I don't remember.

Coughlan: Would you have done
it more than once?

Byrne: I can't recollect.

And those at the receiving end of all this
bounty also had some difficulty remembering.

Michael Lowry, Independent T.D. for
North Tipperary and former Minister for
Transport, Energy and Communication,
was also questioned by John Coughlan.

Coughlan: Nobody in the bank
ever raised the issue of exchange
control with you? Or the necessity of having Central Bank
approval to open a deposit account abroad? Nobody ever
raised that with you?

Lowry: I have no recollection of
that whatsoever.

Mr Bertie Ahern, An Taoiseach and
leader of the Fianna Fáil Party, when asked
what he knew of donations to the Party,
said: 'I – eh – I don't actually remember
talking to Sean Fleming, but on all of these
queries he's the one I'd go to.'

And why not? Mr Fleming was, after
all, the Party Treasurer.

Mr Dermot Ahern T.D. (no relation),
Minister for Social, Community and Family

Affairs, was questioned by Garret Cooney, S.C. for Joseph Murphy Structural Engineers (J.M.S.E.).

> Cooney: Do you recall if the topic of conversation concerned results of the recent election?
> D. Ahern: No.
> Cooney: You don't remember that at all, is it?
> D. Ahern: No.
> Cooney: Your mind is blank?
> D. Ahern: I have no recollection.

Or how about Mr John Ellis T.D.? The man from Manorhamilton Mart who left a number of unpaid debts to farmers in his wake and who was bailed out by the then Taoiseach Mr Haughey, who feared that if Ellis was declared bankrupt the Government would collapse. Ellis was in such a shock at the Boss's generosity that he, too, failed to remember any of it.

Some people – on the other hand – had amazing memories and could remember tiny details and even things that never happened at all. Like Mr Ray Burke, former Minister for Justice and also Foreign Affairs, a man who has handled more brown envelopes in his time than An Post. He told Mr Justice Flood: 'I notice in the transcripts that the word "recollection", "recollect" is used 39 times on the first day and 36 on the second and I think from counting it myself I used the word 30-odd times myself to you.'

Mr James Gogarty, former Director of J.M.S.E., said: 'We are talking now about 11 years ago. I remember it all, I'm telling you, and I have told the Tribunal all the facts.' No amnesia there then.

The Tribunal under Justice Flood was always eventful. There was high drama in the gents' toilet one day when an absent-minded detective forgot his revolver and left the weapon in plain view on the washstand, where it was discovered by Anthony Harris, who was the ex-Assistant City Manager George Redmond's lawyer. Harris left the gun where it was and immediately went to fetch a uniformed Garda.

However, the journalist Sam Smyth clocked that there was something odd going on and followed Harris and the Garda back into the gents'. As soon as Sam pushed open the door the Garda whipped off his cap and put it over the suspicious-looking weapon. But too late. Sam had already seen it and quick as a wink he asked the Guard:

'Is that a gun in your hat, Guard, or are you just happy to see me?'

There was more than a whiff of cordite in the air up the castle yard at the Moriarty Tribunal, which had inherited the smoking gun left over from the McCracken Inquiry. McCracken was set up to investigate alleged payments from Ben Dunne to Mr Michael Lowry (Fine Gael) and Mr Charles Haughey (Fianna Fáil). Ben liked to keep both sides of the political divide happy. The bookies call it spreading your bets.

In his evidence, Ben Dunne said he had been playing golf at Baltray and had three bank drafts in his pocket, each worth £70,000 sterling. As you would when playing a round.

After the game of golf, Mr Dunne phoned Mr Haughey and said he'd call out to see him at his home in Kinsealy. He said he got the impression that Mr Haughey was not himself, but looked down and depressed. As Big Ben was leaving he took the three bank drafts out of his pocket, handed them to Mr Haughey and said: 'Look – that is something for yourself.' And got that much-misquoted reply from the now delighted Mr Haughey: 'Thank you, big fella.'

Mr Haughey, exhibiting the symptoms of full-blown Tribunal amnesia, 'has no recollection' of the post-golf-game bonanza. He accepts, though, that he did in fact receive the bank drafts which were very probably passed on to Des Traynor, who was Haughey's accountant at the time. And the entire £210,000 somehow found its way into the General Account of

Ansbacher Cayman Ltd. From evidence given to McCracken, it would appear that Mr Haughey got in the region of one million pounds from Mr Dunne.

Jerry Healy, Senior Counsel for the Moriarty Tribunal, asked Mr Dunne about this.

> Healy: Can we take it, Mr Dunne, that as an experienced business-man … Can I take it that a million pounds is something you would notice even with the sums of money that went through Dunnes Stores?
>
> Dunne: I … a million pounds in one go I would have noticed a lot quicker, than if it was, excuse the expression, 'on the drip'.
>
> Healy: I know.
>
> Dunne: But I should have noticed it, yes, sir.

What's the odd million here and there to a man who can't remember a twenty million pound sweetheart deal with the taxman?

But it would now appear from the Moriarty Tribunal that Mr Haughey received almost eight and a half million pounds from various sources. Not so much 'on the drip' as a downpour. However, as our esteemed Taoiseach Bertie said of the affair, 'Maybe when you go over eight and a half million you stop getting shocked.'

# 2

# A Trip to the Caymans

Two names emerged from the can of
worms opened at the McCracken Tribunal: Mr Desmond Traynor and Mr
Pauric Collery, whom the Tribunal has
dubbed the 'new' Des Traynor. Des and
Pauric had kept detailed records of the
accounts of the Irish customers of
Ansbacher Cayman Ltd., including those
of Mr Charles Haughey.

However, shortly after the death of Mr
Traynor, a number of such records were
destroyed or taken back to the Cayman
Islands by Mr John Furze. Out of sight, out
of mind and out of the jurisdiction. No
wonder the pirates of the Caribbean buried
their gold there.

Mr Pauric Collery, a Sligoman by birth,
has given evidence that he no longer has

any records relating to the affairs of Charles Haughey. It's probable that such records do exist, either in the files of Ansbacher Cayman Ltd., or in documents held by the late John Furze at the time of his death. Whatever the case, it's unlikely that any paperwork relating to Haughey's involvement will ever see the light of day.

Indeed there were many who were hoping that a lot of incriminating documents might have been cremated with their author, thereby saving the blushes of certain well-heeled members of society. But oh no, some damning documents didn't stay underground – they surfaced again like the dead body in the movie *Deliverance*, still holding that smoking gun.

Fearful that he was under surveillance and that his records of accounts would be stolen, Pauric Collery gave a briefcase full of the coded documents to his secretary, Ms Keogh, for safekeeping. Ms Keogh grew suspicious, however, and through her solicitor passed them on to the Tribunal. Poor old paranoid Pauric, the conscientious accountant, with a secret list of Ansbacher names that read like a Who's Who of Ireland's finest citizens, probably had very good reason to be worried for his own safety.

> Collery: I thought my phone was being tapped. I was ... I was

afraid my house was going to be raided.

John Coughlan S.C.: You wanted to conceal the documents, isn't that right, Mr Collery? To put them beyond the reach of the Tribunal.

Collery: Those records were for my personal protection.

Coughlan: And by giving them to the Tribunal how would you have not been protected? The documents would have been safe and available, isn't that correct?

Collery: I do accept that it was a wrong decision.

Coughlan: Ah come on, Mr Collery, come on. You never told us about any of this, isn't that correct?

Parlous Pauric had also omitted to tell the Tribunal:

- that he'd travelled to the Caymen Islands on the sly

- that he had sorted out the interest on people's offshore accounts

- that he had sent out statements with very dodgy looking letterheads

14

- and that he had handed over £50,000 in a briefcase to Denis Foley T.D.

As Justice Moriarty said of the whole affair: 'Well, Mr Collery, would you accept that this Tribunal would have been barking up a substantially wrong tree if we had not obtained the documents in the briefcase in the most unforeseen of circumstances?'

So there we had the Tribunal barking up the wrong tree, Bertie Ahern like some Mohair-suited eco-warrior up every tree in North Dublin and a millennium tree stuck through every letterbox in the country. Who says money doesn't grow on trees?

The bould Collery was now up to his oxters in it. One politician described his ordeal in the witness box as being 'like watching the lions attack the Christians'. In reality, it was more like watching a bold child sitting on his potty and refusing to let go – for three whole days.

As the cross-examination wore on, Pauric grew redder and redder like a tomato ripening until fit to burst.

But there was even more in store for Collery. Parsimonious Pauric had gone to the Caymans and deducted money from his clients' accounts – without their knowledge – to pay his own litigation costs at the McCracken Tribunal. Again John Coughlan asked him about this.

> Coughlan: Now, there is a critical matter I have to ask you about at this point. There were no deductions made from certain clients, isn't that correct?
>
> Collery: That is correct.
>
> Coughlan: Why was that?
>
> Collery: Well, one of those clients was myself.

The first rule of good creative accounting is 'never leave yourself short'.

In July of 1998, a year after Justice McCracken delivered his report of the findings of the Tribunal, poor old provident Pauric packed his Ambre Solaire and headed off once more to the Cayman Islands to bring the balance of his clients' Ansbacher accounts up to date. He didn't even send a 'wish you were here' postcard to the Tribunal.

> Coughlan: You went and you spent seven days in the Cayman Islands, isn't that right?
>
> Collery: Yes, indeed.
>
> Coughlan: It hardly took you seven days to carry out the exercise did it?
>
> Collery: It took me two and a half days, and the other two and a half days was spent on Seven Mile Beach.

No one asked Pauric to account for the other missing two days. Perhaps he deducted them to cover expenses. For some reason the mathematical abilities of the witnesses and even some of the Tribunal lawyers often leave a lot to be desired.

## MUSICAL INTERLUDE

The following could be sung to the tune of 'Island in the Sun':

Cayman Island in the sun,
With banks discreet for everyone.
Invest my money overseas:
This tax free haven's a home to me

I hope those bankers will resist
Demands to reveal the Ansbacher list.
Though they are very wealthy men
I don't want to be locked up with them.

Oh, island in the sun,
Willed to me by Des Traynor's hand,
All my days I will sing in praise
Of those greedy bankers who run this
    land.

Haughey went on R.T.É.
To say we're fucked financially.
What he failed to tell us then
Was that the nation's wealth was in the
    Cayman.

I see woman on bended knee
Working hard for her family.
I see man with his belt pulled tight.
We were conned by that fiscal shite.

Oh, island in the sun,
Willed to me by Des Traynor's hand,
All my days I will sing in praise
Of those greedy bankers who run this
           land.

# 3

# Hoping against Hope

There was a terrible stink in the Dáil the day the dreaded 'Ansbacher List' hit the fan. First casualty was Denis Foley T.D., personal friend and business associate of property developer and fellow Kerryman John Byrne, who, incidentally, was married to a former Rose of Tralee. Although Mr Foley had known that he had some kind of an offshore account, he had obviously been fervently praying it was not of the Ansbacher variety. Poor Denis told the Tribunal:

> Foley: I had requested statements, but I was shocked when I got the statements.
> John Coughlan S.C.: Well yes … what shocked you about them?

Foley: I was still hoping against hope, because the Tribunal that was set up was to investigate payments to various people, in particular Mr Haughey, and it was a well-known fact that I wasn't a Haughey supporter and we got some correspondence at the time to sign which I had no intention of signing.

Coughlan: I am not dealing with that.

Foley: I just want to make that point. I still believed that there was a hope ...

Coughlan: You believed that?

Foley: I still believed at that stage that I wasn't in Ansbacher. I knew I had an offshore account.

Coughlan: You still believed ...

Foley: I was still hoping.

Coughlan: You were still hoping.

Foley: Yeah.

Coughlan: Now, why did you believe that you weren't in Ansbacher? Give me the reason why you believed that, Mr Foley.

Foley: Well, because when I discussed it with Des Traynor, when I invested that first day, he gave me the name of a company and Des Traynor knew that I, being a politician, should not be in an Ansbacher situation.

Coughlan: An Ansbacher situation was about putting money offshore, clouding its existence, using it in the most secretive way to ensure that it couldn't be discovered, isn't that right?

Foley: That is correct.

Coughlan: And not declaring it to the Revenue authorities in this country by Irish residents. Isn't that what Ansbacher was about, Mr Foley?

Foley: That's correct.

Coughlan: And isn't that what you understood it to be about?

Foley: That is correct.

Coughlan: And you, as a T.D., participating in the business of the House, or as a citizen outside, always understood it to be that?

Foley: That's correct.

Coughlan: Now, you knew you had been dealing with Des Traynor?

Foley: That's right.

Coughlan: You knew your money had not been declared to the Revenue, isn't that right?

Foley: That's right.

Coughlan: You knew that it was offshore?

Foley: That's correct.

Coughlan: And you knew that you had transactions in relation to it which were designed to ensure that it would never be discovered, isn't that correct?

Foley: That is correct.

Coughlan: Armed with those simple pieces of evidence, I must suggest to you that that alone must have caused a question to be raised in your mind that I must be in Ansbacher if Des Traynor is in it and he did all of that, is that right?

Foley: That is correct. Might I add I was still hoping that I was not in Ansbacher.

Coughlan: I understand that.

Foley: I was actually sick of it at the time.

Coughlan: I know. You were worried about it, weren't you?

Foley: I was certainly worried about it.

Coughlan: You were very worried?

Foley: And stressed.

Coughlan: You went into denial about them, did you?

Foley: I certainly did. I certainly did.

Coughlan: Because it was now possible that you could be found out?

Foley: Correct.

Coughlan: And you didn't want to be found out, isn't that right?

Foley: No, I wanted to make my return to the Revenue Commissioners.

Coughlan: You didn't want to be found out that you were in Ansbacher, isn't that right?

Foley: That is correct.

Coughlan: And you never wanted to be found out that you were in Ansbacher, isn't that right?

Foley: That is correct.

Coughlan: And you knew, you knew you were in Ansbacher, isn't that right?

Foley: There was doubt there. I was hoping against hope ...

Coughlan: You knew you were in Ansbacher?

Foley: I don't want to dispute with you now. I want to say I was still hoping against hope that I was not in Ansbacher ...

Before he left the witness box Mr Foley made a point of telling the Tribunal, 'It was a well known fact that I wasn't a supporter of Mr Haughey. When the votes were

23

taking place it was recorded that I voted against him.'

Mr Foley may have forgotten that he had an account in the Cayman Islands, but he certainly was making every effort to put clear blue water between himself and his esteemed former Taoiseach. Joining him in the bid to desert the sinking ship *CJH* was John Byrne, who angrily denied that Charlie Haughey had helped him secure tenants for any of his bunker-like properties. Byrne told the Tribunal that any money he had given indirectly to Haughey was for helicopter flights with Celtic Helicopters, a company run by Haughey's son Ciaran. Byrne himself is an accomplished helicopter pilot, so maybe that's why he never actually availed of Ciaran's services.

Just before he became Taoiseach in 1980 Mr Haughey, with the help of his financial advisor Des Traynor, had a debt of £1.14 million pounds – which he owed to Allied Irish Banks – 'taken care of'. Traynor 'bought' Haughey's loan from A.I.B. and took it into Guinness and Mahon. Haughey was given a £500,000 bank draft. He then met with a senior A.I.B. executive at the Bank's headquarters in Ballsbridge. Haughey never left his car. He handed the draft out the window like spare change for the purchase of a newspaper. The car sped off without a by your leave.

A Mr Phelan, manager of one of the banks dealing with Haughey's finances at the time, wrote to Mr Haughey on his election as Taoiseach in 1980:

> Dear Mr Haughey,
>
> It gives me great pleasure to convey my warmest congratulations on your election to the high offices Leader of Fianna Fáil and An Taoiseach, and to offer you my sincere good wishes for success in both.
>
> To say the task you have taken on is daunting is an understatement, but I have every faith in your ability to succeed in restoring confidence in this great little nation.

However an outstanding debt of £110,000 remained with the bank, which at the time of the Tribunal's initial investigation had not been paid. At one of his last public appearances before the Moriarty Tribunal Mr Haughey was questioned by John Coughlan S.C. about his failure to honour this debt.

> Coughlan: You never paid that, did you?
>
> Haughey: Well, no.
>
> Coughlan: And nobody ... it was recorded as being a debt of

honour, but nonetheless a security was held in respect of the island of Inishvickillaun and nobody asked you to pay that money to honour your debt of honour?

Haughey: No. First of all, the security wasn't of any particular significance in those days and secondly, nobody, nobody – first of all, as well, there was no interest being charged.

Coughlan: There was no interest being charged?

Haughey: And, in fact, I think the letter makes some reference, in fact, that nothing was to happen about it. There were no other – no transactions were to take place, isn't that –

Coughlan: That's right. It was considered a debt of honour and I think what was expected that you, as a man of honour, would honour that debt of honour within a reasonable period of time. I think that could be a reasonable reading of the letter, would you agree?

Haughey: I think you are putting a lot of stress on honour, on the debt of honour, which I don't know what significance the bank attributed to it at that stage, but it's in the letter but they never sought – they never came to me – never mentioned it since and I quite frankly had forgotten about it.

Coughlan: Could I ask you this, you signed and accepted these particular terms, Mr Haughey?

Haughey: Yes.

Coughlan: You were the head of government of this country at the time you did that?

Haughey: Yes.

Coughlan: You held a position of honour, isn't that correct?

Haughey: Yes.

Coughlan: And you were entering into an agreement with this bank to accept a debt of honour, isn't that correct?

Haughey: That's what's in the letter, yes.

Coughlan: And would you agree that a debt of honour is one which would be one would be honoured by honourable people?

Haughey: Yes.

Coughlan: And bearing in mind the position of honour you held, do you have any reason as

to why you didn't honour this
debt?

Haughey: The debt is still there. I
haven't dishonoured it.

With Mr Haughey in the witness box
the Moriarty Tribunal became the hottest
show in town. Special one day passes were
issued, extra seating brought in and TV
monitors set up in rooms off the main
Tribunal chambers for those members of
the public audience who were left outside.
In the castle yard the media circus had
arrived in the shape of satellite TV and
outside broadcast vans. Cameramen film-
ed other cameramen as reporters rabbitted
into microphones and bemused British
journalists wondered aloud: ''Ere – what's
going on?'

Then Mr Haughey's doctors intervened
and the shutters came down. There was to
be no more evidence in public. Mr Haughey
was deemed too ill and too weak to take the
strain of being centre stage. *Hamlet* would
continue, but without the Prince.

Justice Moriarty appointed himself
Commissioner and heard Mr Haughey's
deposition in camera, far from the mad-
dening crowd. For one hour a day, over
twenty days, the barely consenting adults
met in private behind closed doors.

The exchanges were blunt, with Mr
Haughey doing little to conceal his

contempt for John Coughlan. On one occasion Mr Coughlan asked Mr Haughey about how much he knew of Mr Traynor's handling of Haughey's financial affairs. Haughey said he knew nothing. He had just let Traynor 'get on with it' and never asked any questions.

> Coughlan: Ah, Mr Haughey –
> can that be real?
>
> Haughey: There is no 'ah, Mr
> Haughey' about it at all. What
> precise question are you asking
> me?
>
> Coughlan: I am asking you over
> and above that, Mr Haughey,
> whether you had any dis-
> cussion with Mr Traynor?
>
> Haughey: No.
>
> Coughlan: Was your interest not
> even excited to make a ...
>
> Haughey: I refuse to discuss my
> feelings. You keep trying to ask
> me was I surprised? Was I this?
> Was I that? I am here to try and
> ... and I am not in very good
> shape today actually, but I am
> trying to answer the questions
> as best I can and I am not
> interested in going into whether
> I felt that or whether I had ...
> what my emotions were. This is
> a Tribunal, as I understand it,

to establish questions of ... to objectively establish questions of fact. Not my feelings.

Coughlan: Well, I wasn't asking you about your feelings, Mr Haughey.

Haughey: Well you were. You were asking 'was I excited?' Isn't that a feeling?

Coughlan: Was your interest excited?

Haughey: I don't remember.

Coughlan: So can we take it that you weren't even curious as to whether any ...

Haughey: Commissioner, I can't answer these questions, whether I was curious or excited or ... I am excited now, Mr Coughlan.

In *Alice through the Looking Glass* Humpty Dumpty says, 'When I use a word it means just what I choose it to mean, neither more nor less.' Dr Michael Smurfit, chairman of one of the largest companies in Ireland, was clearly a pupil of the Humpty Dumpty School of Linguistics. When he took the stand at the Moriarty Tribunal he used the word 'hypothecating' in his evidence concerning Mr Haughey's requests for money from him. John Coughlan asked Haughey about this.

Haughey: I don't understand what he is saying there by 'hypothecating'. Presumably that's related to the word 'hypothesis', is it?

Coughlan: Yes, I think so.

Haughey: Is there such a verb? But ...

Coughlan: Yes, I see your point Mr Haughey. I think what he meant ...

Haughey: I don't know whether he is hypothecating ...

Coughlan: I think ...

Haughey: ... about the whole matter of the approach or the method of it.

Coughlan: The method, I think, because I think, what he was indicating was ...

Haughey: You are hypothecating now.

But Mr Coughlan pressed on like a latter-day evangelist anxious to enlist Mr Haughey as a disciple to the Tribunal cause.

Coughlan: Would you be prepared to assist the Tribunal to the extent that you yourself might approach people, whom you might speculate about, to see if they made a contribution?

Haughey: You mean I might have done that in the past?

Coughlan: No, no, Mr Haughey. Would you be prepared to do it now, is what I am asking.

Haughey: That I would go out now and approach people?

Coughlan: And ask them ... people ... you might ask them?

Haughey: Not ask them for money?

Coughlan: No.

Haughey: I am sorry we are at total cross-purposes. I thought you were suggesting I ask for money now. Mind you, it wouldn't be a bad idea. But no, I think I see what you are suggesting, that I might now go out and go round and ask people, 'By the way, did you ever subscribe to me in the past?'

Coughlan: Yes.

Haughey: No, I wouldn't be prepared to do that, Mr Coughlan.

They say it is better to give than to receive, and having given over £8 million to Mr Haughey there must have been a whole lot of people out there feeling *so* much better.

All except Mr Mark Kavanagh, that is, who, as the former owner of Captain

America's burger joint, had moved on from fast food to fast money and was now involved with the Irish Financial Services Centre. The Tribunal lawyers were keen to establish whether Mr Haughey had ever received anything from him. No matter how small.

> Coughlan: Did you ever get anything from Mr Mark Kavanagh, to the best of your knowledge?
>
> Haughey: I don't think so. Financial you mean?
>
> Coughlan: Yes.
>
> Haughey: I would be almost categoric [*sic*] in saying no. But ...
>
> Coughlan: Sorry, in fairness, I think can we just deal with that. I think at the opening of the I.F.S.C. or at the launch of the I.F.S.C. you may have been given a small presentation or a present?
>
> Haughey: Money?
>
> Coughlan: No, no, no, no. I think it might have been a small bit of silver or something of that nature, but that is not a matter of interest to the Tribunal. I am just saying that you received a small present from Mr

Kavanagh on behalf of the developers.

Haughey: I don't even remember that to be honest with you. I don't remember even ... I'm sorry but I don't even remember the opening of the I.F.S.C. I should because it was, as I said before, it was a major, major thing in Irish financial economic life. But to be quite frank, I just do not remember. Did it take place down ...?

Coughlan: I think it may have been a silver trowel or something like that.

Haughey: My house is full of them. Architects and builders nearly always give you a silver trowel for some reason best known to themselves on these occasions.

## ANOTHER MUSICAL INTERLUDE

The following could be sung to the tune of 'They Can't Take That Away from Me':

They're gonna take your shirts
By Charvet of Paris.
They don't care if it hurts.
No, no – they can't take that away from me.

34

They're gonna seize your yacht,
No more Coq Hardi.
They'll impound the whole lot.
No, no they can't take that away from
    me.

We may never see his likes again
In Inisvickillaun.
Even Thatcher's teapot he may have to
    pawn.

Winning the Tour de France,
And the Rose of Tralee,
The GUBU utterance –
No – they can't take that away from me.

You're no longer the boss.
No P.J. Mara on your knee.
But you couldn't give a toss –
No – they can't take that away from me.

# 4

# A Bevy of Bovales

Katie Hannon, the political Correspondent with the *Examiner*, was once asked what she thought the difference was between the Moriarty and the Flood Tribunals. She answered: 'Well, the Moriarty Tribunal is like the Loreto Convent where the girls are well behaved, well turned out and go strictly by the rules, whereas the Flood Tribunal is a bit like the "tech". It's all over the place – anything goes – but you know the crack is going to be so much better.'

In a way the Flood Tribunal was a bit like a soap opera – *Emmerdale* or *Fair City* – where we came to know and love the same characters who turned up day after day. Like the brothers Tom and Mick Bailey of Bovale Developments. They should be given shares in Kodak, they have been photographed so often going into Dublin Castle.

The Bailey brothers were originally of farming stock from County Roscommon. They had left school after basic primary education and at an early age went into the building trade. They were industrious, hard-working young men who built to high specifications and standards. As their reputation for quality housing grew so too did their business. They expanded into developing new housing estates in a small way but gradually, through good business acumen and a few shrewd deals, they were building up a substantial land bank of prime north Dublin real estate, which they were quite keen to have re-zoned from agricultural and light industrial to high-density housing. They went about this in time-honoured fashion – by buying people drink.

More at home on a building site than in the witness box, they are plain-speaking men who tell it like it is and are more than a match for any lawyer.

Counsel for the Flood Tribunal, Des O'Neill, asked Mick Bailey about lobbying of Dublin County Councillors at their meetings – and then doing a bit of follow up work in a different, more relaxed venue afterwards.

O'Neill: You would have been considered, I take it, a very hospitable person in those venues – meeting the night's bill for drinks for councillors, isn't that right?

M. Bailey: No, I would, if ... I would buy a drink for people, out of courtesy, no question about it.

O'Neill: Well, in effect, were you running an open bar for the councillors in Conway's pub?

M. Bailey: I was not running an open bar in Conway's pub. Jesus Christ, what's wrong with you?

O'Neill: You were meeting the bill at the end of the evening, Mr Bailey, isn't that so?

M. Bailey: I would have contributed, if there was a bar there. I would say, people supported me – or if they didn't support me, ones that didn't support me ... [At this point Mr O'Neill looked knowingly towards the Press Gallery] You can be laughing at the press there – I am talking to you, Mr O'Neill. If you don't mind me saying, I think you are playing to the gallery again.

Mick Bailey and Des O'Neill are as unalike as any two people can be. In boxing terms it was like big Mike Tyson versus little Barry McGuigan. Whenever the two men step into the arena together they are perfect gentlemen. When they trade punches, they always say, 'Sorry – did that hurt?' Just take a look at what happened when O'Neill questioned Mick Bailey about a list of political contributions the Baileys had made over the years.

> O'Neill: In dealing with the payments that were made by your company and yourself, which are recorded over the years in the list which you provided to the Tribunal today, Mr Bailey, it would appear that in the year 1997 you paid a sum of £14,100 in total in political contributions; isn't that so?
>
> M. Bailey: If that is what the figure says.
>
> O'Neill: That is a question of mathematics?
>
> M. Bailey: I didn't make it up. If you want me to make it up I will try to make it up, but I didn't.
>
> O'Neill: The tots that I have made from the list that you have provided here are as follows: in

1989 you contributed £1,200.
In 1992, £800. In 19–

M. Bailey: Hold on a second,
what did you say, 1989?

O'Neill: We will start at the
beginning. 1989: £1,200?

M. Bailey: Yes.

O'Neill: 1992: £800?

M. Bailey: Yeah.

O'Neill: 1995: £5,800?

M. Bailey: One second, now. 1 –
2 – 4 – 5,000 – £4,800; that is
right.

[Here the witness did some
totting up.]

O'Neill: £5,800 is what I have
now.

M. Bailey [more totting]: 'Four
and four is eight. Then two and
two is four–

O'Neill [having also done some
totting]: Sorry … £4,800.

M. Bailey: I wouldn't like to be
catching you out now.

O'Neill: My fault entirely.

M. Bailey: We are all human,
thank God.

O'Neill: We are all human,
indeed.

M. Bailey: I don't see much of it
though, not on this side of the
house anyway.

O'Neill: We are not that hard on you, Mr Bailey.

M. Bailey: I appreciate you have a job to do, the same as I have; and I respect you for it.

Those present at the Tribunal took this last remark with a *very* large grain of salt. However, Mr O'Neill remained his implacable Sphinx-like self.

Anyone who has been to a Court of Law will know how solemn the occasion can be. The strict protocol and gravity of the subject matter adds to the air of tension, and anything that breaks that tension usually produces howls of laughter. The following incident almost had the entire Press Gallery thrown out of the Tribunal.

Mick's brother Tom is the other half of the formidable Bailey duo. Tom is a mountain of a man with a great shock of curly hair and the look of someone who would much rather be at a cattle mart than the Tribunal.

It happened during Des O'Neill's cross-examination of Tom Bailey, who was being questioned in a general way about where he worked and lived.

O'Neill: You said that you moved to Meath in 1986, and yesterday your wife talked about a specialised farming operation that you are carrying on. Can you elaborate on that please?

T. Bailey: I breed purebred Suffolk sheep.

O'Neill: I see.

T. Bailey: And some purebred cattle as well.

O'Neill: Perhaps you will tell me what's the size of it?

T. Bailey: Well, the farm I lived on at that stage was 25 acres but some of the sheep would be pretty expensive.

O'Neill: I see. What price would those sheep be around that time approximately?

T. Bailey: I know in 1989 I gave £58,000 for 16 sheep at a sale in Scotland.

O'Neill: For 16?

T. Bailey: And I bought – sorry, I bought a stock ram the same year as well for 10,000 sterling guineas. And I have given as much as 94,000 punts for a sheep.

At which point a journalist in the Press Gallery whispered, 'Jaysus, and he only paid thirty grand for Ray Burke. They must have seen him coming.'

And one wonders if that is how Ray Burke acquired the nickname 'Rambo'.

Tom's wife Caroline Bailey, who also acted as company bookkeeper, gave evidence to the Tribunal too. Caroline was asked, again by Des O'Neill S.C., how Tom and Mick paid themselves out of Bovale accounts. (This, by the way, concerns the accounts ledger that came to be known at the Tribunal as the 'pussy book' because of the cute picture of a kitten on the cover.)

> C. Bailey: I don't know how they do it. As I have said several times I am sure they have a trust – they can talk between themselves. I don't know how they do it.
>
> O'Neill: Well how would they work out, for example, the Weir's payment of £23,000, which is made in December 1997; what was that payment for?
>
> C. Bailey: It was for jewellery.
>
> O'Neill: It was for jewellery. Was it to be shared between Tom and Michael, or otherwise? It was for one or the other?
>
> C. Bailey: Which? The jewellery? I am sorry, can you repeat it?
>
> O'Neill: The £23,000 was spent in Weir's on jewellery?
>
> C. Bailey: Yes.
>
> O'Neill: Does one brother get the benefit of that, or the other?
>
> C. Bailey: I got the benefit of that.

O'Neill: You got the benefit. So presumably that is attributable to Tom?

C. Bailey: I hope so.

O'Neill: So Michael has to get £13,000 ... half of that ... £11,500 pounds of a credit.

C. Bailey: Yes: I appreciate that, yes.

O'Neill: How is that done?

C. Bailey: I don't know how they do it.

O'Neill: You don't.

C. Bailey: No. I am not interested. Why would I be? Didn't I get the jewellery?

For a couple of rough diamonds the Bailey boys were worth over 40 million quid, but did they let all that wealth go to their heads? No sir, they kept all their records of accounts in an old shipping container on a building site in Finglas ... which strangely burned out on the very day the Supreme Court ordered them to hand over the said documents to the Tribunal. Talk about a coincidence. Well the lawyers did – for nearly *two* days; and poor old Tom and Mick had to foot the bill. A bill which eventually topped two million pounds.

Tom Bailey was questioned by Mr John Gallagher, Senior Counsel for the Flood Tribunal, as to whether or not he was present at the scene of the fire on the morning it occurred.

Gallagher: Did any employee of Bovale have documents stored in the hut that you are aware of?

T. Bailey: No. There was some hats and some clothes all right.

Gallagher: Now, the District Officer, Mr Doyle, gave evidence here. He said in the course of his evidence on Day 159, that when he was at the scene of the fire he was approached by a man who was introduced to him by a fireman as a builder, and who had expressed concern. He then goes on at a later stage to describe the person then as having a country accent, among other things.

T. Bailey: This is the man that went on to say that 'my recollection of him would be a stocky man'.

Gallagher: That's correct.

T. Bailey: I don't think you could regard me as a 'stocky man'.

Gallagher: Well, he described ... he also described the man in question as 'a country man'?

T. Bailey: Well, there is lots of country people working in Dublin.

45

Gallagher: Indeed Mr Bailey.

T. Bailey: Mmm. Including yourself, Mr Gallagher.

Gallagher: And he also described the individual as having 'a country accent who was wearing a cap'?

T. Bailey: I don't wear a cap.

Gallagher: And had a better head of hair than he had?

T. Bailey: Okay. I don't wear a cap. I don't wear a cap anyway. There is no question about it. I wasn't there anyway, Mr Gallagher.

At which point Colm Allen, Senior Counsel for the Baileys, leapt to his feet.

Allen: Sir – this is precisely the point that I was making in relation to this. I mean, if Mr Gallagher wants to come straight out and say: 'you torched the place on the morning of the appeal because you were worried about the outcome of the appeal', then he should do so. Let him put his ... let him put his cards on the table. I also suggest, sir, that on the issue of the cap – that if you put a cap on Mr Bailey you will find that his hair doesn't curl up around it, as the gentleman who ...

Flood: We won't go into sartorial
   elegance at this time.
[Slight pause.]
Allen: That is hirsute elegance,
   not sartorial elegance.

Is that what they call a moot point?

ANOTHER MUSICAL INTERLUDE
The following could be sung to the air of
'Bill Bailey':

Bovale Homes and Baileys,
Those Bailey Boys,
They moan the whole Tribunal long.
We cooked the books honey!
We paid ourselves.
We know we done the State some wrong.

Remember that fire in Finglas when it
   burned out
Leaving nothing but ashes and foam?
You know we ain't to blame.
We never lit that flame.
Yes, they're the Bailey Boys from
   Bovale Homes.

Won't you cop on you Baileys?
Won't you cop on?
Down on the farm's where you belong.
Tom's into Suffolk sheep,
Mick bought a horse.
Just country boys all along.

47

Remember those boozy nights down in
    Conway's pub
When those councillors just wouldn't
    go home?
While they were getting pissed
Tom and Mick kept a list
Of the cheques from Bovale Homes.

Don't you phone home you Baileys,
Don't you phone home.
They've got you taped at Telecom.
When we phoned Psychics Live
To find out our fate
They'd got it all on CD Rom.

Remember all those times you rang Ray
    Burke?
They've been through it with a fine-
    tooth comb.
They know that we were ringing
Just to hear Ray singing:
Put your sweet lips a little closer to the
    phone.
Well the light's on, but there ain't
    nobody home.

# 5

# Mr Gogarty Comes to Town

Ahhh, money … Don't you just love the feel of it and the smell of it? The foldiness of it, the crispness of all those new notes? The reassuring warmth of a whole wad of it close to your heart in your wallet, or tucked into your inside breast pocket.

Well, in 1989, just to put things in perspective, the average industrial wage in Ireland was £10,800 a year. The price of a pint was £1.45. You could have bought a family car for £6,500 and you could have, believe it or not, bought a house in Dublin 4 for £30,000.

Yes indeedy – £30,000. The same as the disputed amount of money paid over to

49

Mr Ray Burke in 1989 in a brown paper envelope.

And the man who blew the whistle on the whole payments for planning affair was the irrepressible Mr James Gogarty. He who told the Tribunal: 'I'm just trying to get at the truth, warts and all. But don't worry, it will all come out in the washing so it will, warts and all.'

Ah, yes – the most memorable character ever to grace a witness box in legal history. The man Colm Allen, Senior Counsel for the Baileys, described as the Tribunal's star witness. To which Gogarty replied: 'If you put any more stars on me I'll be flying so I will. Stars and stripes and feathers.'

And the man who – to paraphrase justice Flood – 'spent forty days wandering like an Arab in the desert before eventually – like the snail – he eventually reached Jerusalem'.

Now, let's go back in time, to that famous, or should we say infamous, trip to Mr Ray Burke's house. On that fateful day in June, the date of which no one who was there can remember but could well be Bloomsday for all we know, there were so many characters wandering around Dublin with brown paper envelopes full of money in their pockets.

Mr Murphy, mentioned in the following extract, was the third part of the terrible trio travelling in the car. Sometimes referred to as 'Junior' he, along with Gogarty, was there as a representative of Joseph Murphy Structural Engineering.

Mr John Gallagher for the Flood Tribunal questioned Mr Gogarty about the journey but didn't seem to be getting to the nub of the matter quickly enough for Gogarty.

> Gogarty: I know you solicitors are getting well paid for this – thirteen hundred or thirteen hundred and fifty a day – but would you ever get on with it for God's sake, you're giving me a pain in the face, so you are.
>
> Gallagher: All right. Now, Mr Gogarty, who drove the car to the meeting in Swords with Mr Burke?
>
> Gogarty: Mr Bailey. It was a Mercedes, a dark grey Mercedes.
>
> Gallagher: Where did Mr Murphy sit?
>
> Gogarty: He sat in the front with Mr Bailey.
>
> Gallagher: And where did you go when you got to Swords?
>
> Gogarty: Well, I sat in the back of the car and Junior was in the front of it, and I had the envelope in my pocket and we

were going along, and I don't
think there was a whole lot said,
but I said that ... I remember
saying that ... would we get a
receipt for the money, and
Bailey said: 'Will we, fuck.'

Later on at the Tribunal Mr Colm Allen
for the Baileys brought up the topic while
cross-examining Mr Gogarty:

Allen: You allege that Mr Michael
Bailey said, if you excuse the
rather rugged language: 'Will
we, fuck.'
Gogarty: That's right.
Allen: I presume, Mr Gogarty,
that it wasn't an invitation.
[The rather packed public
gallery exploded with belly
laughter at this point much to
Gogarty's consternation, as he
thought for a moment that
Colm Allen had scored a legal
point against him.]
Gogarty: I beg your pardon?
Allen: What?
Gogarty: What is all the laughing
about?
Allen: I don't know, Mr Gogarty,
it certainly escapes my attention
– there has been a great deal of
laughing in this hall for the past
four weeks, six weeks.

Gogarty: I don't know what you're getting at.

Allen: Do you seriously ask this Tribunal to accept that you actually conceived of getting a receipt from a Government minister whom you were seeking to bribe?

Gogarty: Yes, I was. I have told you that, yes.

Allen: What did you think he was going to do, Mr Gogarty? Was he going to sort of lean behind him and take down this bribery and corruption receipt book for Fingal County Council matters and write out a receipt: 'Received from James Gogarty for bribery and corruption – £30,000?'

Gogarty: I can't speak for Mr Burke.

Allen: You wanted a receipt for a bribe?

Gogarty: I expected a response.

Allen: You wanted a receipt for a bribe, is that what you are telling us, Mr Gogarty?

Gogarty: Yes. But I don't know what you are trying to get at you know, because it's fairly straight.

Allen: Don't worry about what I am 'trying to get at', Mr Gogarty.

Gogarty: I am, because you told me I am going to be ambushed.

Allen: Never fear, Mr Gogarty. 'Ambush' suggests an element of surprise, wouldn't that be correct?

Gogarty: That would be correct.

Allen: May I take it that you cannot be ambushed if you are told of something which you already know? Do you understand that as a fairly basic concept?

Gogarty: I would have to think about it.

Allen: Think away, Mr Gogarty.

Gogarty: Would you repeat it for me again?

Allen: Certainly. So you can think twice?

Gogarty: Yes.

Allen: Would you accept that you cannot be ambushed if something is put to you about yourself and your conduct of which you already have knowledge because there is no element of surprise involved in such an exercise?

Gogarty: I don't know, because the use of language is a dangerous thing. The use of the English language, you know, it is a dangerous thing.

Just how dangerous Mr Allen would find out later in the proceedings. Mr Allen complained that he couldn't carry out a proper cross-examination of the witness with Gogarty's counsel 'up and down like the bloomers of a member of one of the oldest professions in the world'.

Now this was at the end of a long day of legal argument, and the following morning Colm Allen apologised for demeaning a fellow member of the bar counsel. About twenty minutes later, when Allen was again cross-examining Gogarty, he called him Mr Bailey by mistake and quickly said, 'I'm sorry – it's Mr Gogarty!' Gogarty looked at him for a moment like a cat toying with a mouse and said, 'Is that another one of your bloomers?'

Again the public gallery rocked with laughter. Gogarty had rallied with an ace and for once Colm Allen had got his knickers in a twist.

By mid-summer of 1999 photographers and journalists outnumbered tourists by two to one in Dublin Castle as Mr Ray Burke, formerly Minister for Justice and also Foreign Affairs, took the stand.

Mr Burke was cross-examined by Mr Frank Callanan, Senior Counsel for James Gogarty. Mr Callanan asked Ray Burke about what happened to the £30,000 so-called 'donation' made to Fianna Fáil by Gogarty on behalf of J.M.S.E.

> Callanan: Mr Burke, I think you accept that you did not advise Fianna Fáil that you had received a political donation of £30,000 from J.M.S.E.?
>
> Burke: That's correct.
>
> Callanan: We are not talking here about a couple of hundred pounds or a couple of thousand pounds, we are talking about a payment of £30,000, Mr Burke?
>
> Burke: That's true.
>
> Callanan: So that we can take it that J.M.S.E. would not have received a Christmas card from you, from your party leader or from the Treasurer of Fianna Fáil?
>
> Burke: I don't know whether they received a Christmas card from anybody, but they didn't get one. I didn't send them one.

By a strange coincidence, around the time that Mr Gogarty and his entourage had journeyed like the Three Wise Men bearing gifts to the Minister, Mr Burke had also received another donation of £30,000 from a company called Rennicks. Rennicks is a subsidiary company in a group called

Fitzwilton, which is owned by Sir Tony O'Reilly. At that time O'Reilly wanted to set up a television line rental company in Ireland. However, in many rural areas local groups had set up their own television 'deflector' systems which provided almost free multichannel TV viewing to its members. O'Reilly wanted the 'illegal deflector' systems wiped out and Ray Burke was the Minister for Telecom-munications who could implement the laws to ban these systems. However, it was a political hot potato and no one wanted to take away a freebie from the electorate. The Rennicks payment of £30,000 to Ray Burke somehow got pushed onto the back burner at the Flood Tribunal and once mentioned it quickly disappeared off the radar screen.

However, the Fianna Fáil party heard about this Rennicks donation and went looking for their pound of flesh. And what they got was a bank draft for just £10,000 that Mr Burke brought with him to an election lunch in the Westbury Hotel.

> Burke: Again, my recollection of the – of what happened – was that at some stage over the lunch the – what I had presented must have been looked at – must have been – the scale of it was looked at, and

> at some stage on my way out
> one or other said to me 'our
> understanding is that you got
> more', and I said 'that's as much
> as you are getting, good luck'.

Since then the Tribunal has established that Mr Burke had over £100,000 in political donations stashed away 'on behalf of' the Fianna Fáil Party. As Mr Burke sat in the witness box beating his breast and making a virtue of the fact that he had kept a hundred grand in 'safe keeping' for Fianna Fáil for twenty years, Mr Hanratty reminded Ray that he had once been Minister for Justice.

> Hanratty: Did you think you were
> above the law?
> Burke: Never.

Almost all of the witnesses appearing before the Tribunals have had some difficulty in remembering certain events. Such as who gave them money, where it was handed over, how much was in the brown paper envelope – minor details like that.

But Mr Burke was the first witness to remember exactly what he did with £15,000 he withdrew in cash from a bank in Jersey. He described the money trail precisely. However, unfortunately for Ray, none of the tale he told the Tribunal was true. Mr Hanratty took up the story.

Hanratty: What I suggest to you, Mr Burke, is that that is not simply an error in recollection in the sense that you failed to recall something. You appear to have recalled something that didn't actually happen. You said that you put it into your safe in Dublin, that you had withdrawn it for on-going political expenses and that you subsequently changed your mind about that – rather as in having changed your mind about lighting the fire, you decided to bring coal back to Newcastle. Having changed your mind, you took it out of your safe, put it in a bag, took it on an aeroplane over to London – admitting en route a breach of exchange control legislation – went via London to Jersey, brought the money, not to your bank in Jersey, but to Mr Wheeler in Bedell Cristin, and handed over the money to Mr Wheeler in cash. Mr Burke, it's one thing not to remember something. But I suggest to you, to remember things which didn't actually occur at all is a very odd kind of failure of recollection. Did you dream it up?

Burke: No, I didn't dream it up
but obviously my mind has
played games with me in
relation to it, Mr Hanratty.

Hanratty: How could you possibly sit there with a straight
face and tell this Tribunal that
all of this, all of that complicated, detailed story was a
failure of recollection?

But of course it was second nature for
Mr Burke to sit there with a straight face
and tell porkies. He once informed the Dáil
that 'all contributions I received were
during the course of General Election
campaigns and not in between them'.

And when Ray told the Dáil that the
£30,000 from Gogarty was the largest
donation he had ever received, he somehow
forgot to mention the other £30,000 he got
from Fitzwilton. The £35,000 from Oliver
Barry. The £50,000 from Kalabraki. And
let's not forget the £60,000 he received
from the builder Joe McGowan in 1984.
But as Ray proudly said of the donations,
'They were given to me as the standard
bearer of Fianna Fáil.' Some standard.

Mr Joe Finnegan was one of the legal
representatives who defended Mr Burke
during the early stages of the Tribunal.
Despite Mr Finnegan's best endeavours on
behalf of his client Mr Burke, the Tribunal

found that Burke had indeed accepted a corrupt payment from Bailey, Murphy Jnr. and Gogarty in Briargate, Burke's residence in 1989. And further it also stated that Mr Burke's house in Swords amounted to a corrupt payment and was given to him by Mr Tom Brennan and his associates. Despite these findings against him Mr Burke submitted a legal bill of £10 million to the Tribunal which he expected the taxpayers of Ireland to pay on his behalf. His application to have his fees paid by the State was rejected on the grounds that he deliberately obstructed the Tribunal.

During his final stint in the witness box, Mr Burke was examined by Patricia Dillon, Senior Counsel for the Flood Tribunal. Ms Dillon has been described by a journalist as: 'Anne Robinson with serious attitude'. But instead of dismissing Burke as the weakest link she told him: 'I suggest to you, Mr Burke, that if you are prepared to lie about little things, you might just as easily lie about big things.'

Mr Burke went through the roof and, when he had finished giving his evidence, he told some members of the press just what he thought of his new interrogator. He said: 'You know, that woman reminds me of the story of the man who never spoke to his wife in all the years of their married life. He was asked why he had kept silent for so long and his reply was: "I haven't been able to get a fucking word in edgeways from day one.'"

And from day one, Jim Gogarty has insisted that Ray got rather more than he admits to.

> Gogarty: I am satisfied that there was £40,000 in the envelope that Junior passed over, and that I had passed over. And I assumed that Bailey's envelope contained £40,000. Now there could have been feathers in it for all I know, but that's the way I looked at it.
>
> John Gallagher, Senior Counsel for the Flood Tribunal: So far as you are concerned, what was the total amount handed over on that occasion to Mr Burke?
>
> Gogarty: I thought between the two – the three of us – we handed over £80,000, £80,000.

Eighty grand? Not bad for a day's work.

The politicians may have reaped the harvest at the time, but it's pretty plain who's bringing home the very prime bacon now: the lawyers. At that time in 2000 there were 9 judges and more than 200 lawyers employed by various tribunals. In this day and age a Senior Counsel receives a 'brief' fee of €32,000 and 'refreshers' of €2,000 a day, and for part days they get €200 per hour. Over the past six years what is the total cost of the Tribunals? €190 million. And rising.

Who would have thought the law would become the new rock and roll!

But make no mistake – these are, of course, the best lawyers and judges that money can buy.

# 6

# A funny Thing Happened on the Way to the Tribunal

The Flood Tribunal has been called a 'Frankenstein spiralling out of control', but it could often be more like the Mad Hatter's Tea Party, as this transcription of one of the more surreal cross-examinations of the whole proceedings shows.

Things get curiouser and curiouser by the minute as Counsel for the Flood Tribunal – Mr Des O'Neill as the Mad Hatter – asks the March Hare, Michael Bailey, to explain to him what thirty grand in an envelope might look like.

O'Neill: You saw the transaction of the hand-over, is that right?

M. Bailey: That is correct.

O'Neill: And were these packages handed over individually, or were they both handed over together?

M. Bailey: They were handed over together.

O'Neill: And can you describe, insofar as you can, the approximate size of either of these two packages?

M. Bailey: They were ... I would say they were brown envelopes, and about 9 inches by 7 inches – or maybe 9 by 9 – that type of a brown business-type envelope.

O'Neill: Yes. Were they both the same bulk?

M. Bailey: I can't recall that.

O'Neill: Were they both the same size – if empty, put it that way?

M. Bailey: I believe they were.

O'Neill: And how bulky were they?

M. Bailey: They seemed reasonably bulky, I thought.

O'Neill: The envelopes you are telling us about are 9 by 9, and quite bulky?

M. Bailey: That's correct.

O'Neill: By reference to, say, the size of a 9-inch brick, can you say how thick they would have been?

M. Bailey: To a 9-inch brick?

O'Neill: Yes.

M. Bailey: Is there such a thing?

O'Neill: Well, you tell me. I am not a builder.

M. Bailey: I never seen a 9-inch brick.

O'Neill: It's a 9-inch block, isn't it? Is there a 9-inch block, Mr Bailey?

M. Bailey: 9 inches by 9 inches? You know – there is a 9-inch block but it's not a 9 by 9 block. It's a 9 by 4 block and if this one – this might be a 9 by 2 block. I am not being – I am trying to ...

O'Neill: I am just wondering how thick it was.

M. Bailey: I think it was probably about a 9 by 2 block of a brown bag.

O'Neill: And is that the sum total of both or ...

M. Bailey: That's my recollection, a 9 by 2 – if you want to put it into – that's a new one to me.

O'Neill: Is that the content of one envelope or the contents of two?

M. Bailey: I believe it was the two.

O'Neill: The two would have totalled that?

M. Bailey: The two would be two 9 by 2s.

O'Neill: Two 9 by 2s?

M. Bailey: Blocks, yeah ...

O'Neill: So the size of a 9 by 4 then in total, which is a block, as far as I know?

M. Bailey: If you want – well, we'll say a 9 by 4, cut in two.

Jim Gogarty and his arch nemesis, Mr Garret Cooney, Counsel for J.M.S.E., Gogarty's old employer, were like two gladiators stepping into the arena each day, with no quarter given and none expected. This is what took place when Garret Cooney was cross-examining Mr Gogarty and Gogarty refused to give a straight-forward answer.

Cooney: Can I just intervene for a moment to say, Mr Chairman, it must by now be abundantly clear that Mr Gogarty has adopted a technique to avoid the point of the questions by giving long rambling speeches from the dock. Now again I respectfully ask ...

Gogarty: From the dock! Oh

> Jesus – I didn't know that ... I
> didn't know that ...
> Cooney: From the witness box.
> Gogarty: I'm in the dock! You
> said it, and ...
> Cooney: This is breaching
> proportions, Mr ...
> Gogarty: Putting me in the dock!
> Oh, Mother of God, put me in
> the dock.

Mr Gogarty could on occasion give vent to rather passionate outbursts from the witness box and his favourite refrain – or, indeed, ejaculation – was 'Oh, Jesus!'

This phrase caused some concern to listeners when it was used on the nightly re-enactments of the Tribunal on *Tonight with Vincent Browne*. Eventually Mr Gogarty went an ejaculation too far, as it were, and a female listener rang the show to complain.

> Female listener: Hello. I'm phon-
> ing to say that I love your
> programme, but it upsets me to
> hear that man using the Holy
> Name in vain every night.
> Could you not leave it out
> altogether?

The producer explained that the nightly re-enactments were taken verbatim from the Tribunal transcripts and what a witness

said in evidence that day is what had to be
faithfully reproduced in all fairness.

> Female listener: Oh yes, I know
> that – but could you not put in a
> 'bleep' every time Mr Gogarty
> uses the Holy Name?
> Producer: But if we did that, the
> listeners might think that the
> man was saying 'fuck' all the
> time.

Mishearing what has been said at the
Tribunal is a common occurrence and this
was especially so in relation to Justice
Flood, who used expressions that seemed
to belong to another age. One day Mr
Cooney asked to examine a newly discovered document and Justice Flood told
him, 'Certainly, Mr Cooney. You may bite
the shilling to test its worth.'

A junior reporter from RTÉ who had
obviously been born after the introduction
of decimalisation asked in all seriousness:
'What did Flood mean by telling Cooney
that he could bite his shins to see if it hurt?'

This particular junior reporter has gone
on to become one of RTÉ's 'hot properties' and, as the saying goes, he is
certainly not short of a bob if he now ever
wants to bite it and test its worth.

# 7

# Show Me the Money

Ray Burke wasn't the only recipient of one
of those ubiquitous brown paper envelopes
in circulation at the time. James Gogarty
and the Baileys' Senior Counsel, Colm
Allen, had quite a heated set to over a
disputed payment of £50,000 pounds
from the Baileys to Gogarty.

Gogarty claimed that Bailey gave him
the money and told him to forget about his
row with the Murphys and enjoy life; while
the Baileys claimed that the fifty grand was
part payment of a finder's fee for land that
Gogarty had demanded upfront.

Colm Allen questioned Mr Gogarty
about the post-dated cheque for £50,000
which was given to him by Bailey in the
Skylon Hotel.

Allen: You have told us that Mr Bailey, presumably to your surprise, approached your person and put or stuck or stuffed into your top pocket, an envelope, the contents of which you were unaware; is that correct?

Gogarty: That's correct.

Allen: Was it a sealed envelope?

Gogarty: I think it was now.

Allen: And you say that you made no comment to Mr Bailey, that you went home and that you opened the envelope and found that it contained a cheque for £50,000?

Gogarty: That's correct.

Allen: You also say that the Baileys did not owe you any money at the time?

Gogarty: That's correct.

Allen: And there was no valid reason why this cheque should have been offered to you?

Gogarty: That's correct.

Allen: That being the case, Mr Gogarty, why did you not immediately return the cheque to Mr Bailey?

Gogarty: I held on to it.

Allen: That's not the question I asked you. Why did you not

immediately return this un-solicited cheque for £50,000 – a considerable sum, I am sure you will agree – why did you not return it to Mr Bailey?

Gogarty: I didn't see any necessity to return it. I didn't cash it, I kept it.

Allen: I see. Surely it was quite an extraordinary incident.

Gogarty: It was.

Allen: But you, if you are to be believed, did absolutely nothing about it?

Gogarty: I did.

Allen: Well, we know you put it in a tin, in a tin box; is that what you mean when you say that you did something about it?

Gogarty: Well, I kept it as a keep-sake.

Allen: You kept it as a keepsake?

Gogarty: Yes. It is grand to look at an odd time, you know?

Allen: And that's your sworn evidence, Mr Gogarty, as to why you kept it?

Gogarty: That's my sworn evidence.

Allen: 'It was grand to look at it every now and then.'

Gogarty: Yes.

Allen: 'As a keepsake.'

Gogarty: Like an old photo-
graph, you know. If I had one of
you I would keep it too as well.

A self-made man and multi-millionaire,
the builder Tom Brennan, who is now
resident in the Isle of Man, kept a low
profile and, despite his vast wealth, never
lost his strong Mayo accent or what some
might call his 'cute hoor' charm. Tom
shunned all publicity and kept well out of
the spotlight. That is, until he tripped
himself up over donations he made to Ray
Burke and was grilled like a kipper in the
witness box. Tom maintained that any
donations made to Burke were as a result
of fundraising activities in Britain. Post
race-meeting dinners were organised and
people who may never have heard of Mr
Burke were handing over wads of cash.
Justice Flood was curious about this and
had earlier asked Ray: 'What did you do?
Hand round a plate after the dessert? No, I
suppose nothing as vulgar as that.'

Meanwhile Tom was asked to produce
documents of accounts to the Tribunal. Mr
Patrick Hanratty, for the Flood Tribunal,
then questioned him thus:

Hanratty: Have you been given
any indication then when
we'll have this information?
Brennan: Oh, I haven't. No.

Obviously, we have to see what …

Hanratty: Well, will we have it before the conclusion of the Tribunal's work?

Brennan: Depends on when that will be.

Hanratty: About three years' time.

Brennan: Oh, you should have it before that.

So Tom the high-flyer set off to collect the documents in person.

Brennan: I rang the travel agent's and I booked a flight to Jersey … or to the Isle of Man … yesterday morning. I went on the flight yesterday morning. [Ladies and Gentlemen, fasten your seatbelts. You're in for a bumpy ride!] We left Dublin about … we left at 8.20 on the flight but we couldn't leave because of the fog on the Isle of Man and we left at 9:20. When we got to the Isle of Man the fog had receded for a while and then returned. And we … he said: 'We can't land … we have enough juice for an hour.' So we were flown around the island for an hour, and then he decided: 'We can't land. I have to go to Liverpool.' When we got to Liverpool, we landed there, and this is nearly twelve. And I said, 'What is the chances?' He said: 'We won't go back until this fog lifts but you could be okay by two or three o'clock.' I said: 'That's no good because all my people are there.' So I got a flight from Liverpool and came home [i.e. to Dublin] myself. There is no point going back to the Isle of Man, because if I landed in the Isle of Man and I couldn't get out, I wouldn't be here today.

Mr Justice Flood described Tom the builder's tale as 'a concatenation of circumstances, a unique situation which seems to be clouded in fog'.

Tom Brennan wasn't the only – shall we say – 'eccentric' witness at the Tribunal. Jim Gogarty's old comrade-in-arms from his days in Taca (that's the Garda Siochana reserves from the forties, by the way, not the fundraisers and friends of Fianna Fáil from the seventies), Joseph Murphy Senior, also had a rather intriguing background that was unearthed by a reporter from the *Examiner* newspaper.

It seems that Joe Murphy was christened John Murphy, but changed his name to Joe when he went to the UK. Whereas Joe Murphy's brother John had been christened James, but James changed his name to John when John became Joe.

No wonder the Tribunal is taking years to sort it all out.

A fellow Kerryman and long-time friend of Joe Murphy's, Mr Bat O'Shea, also gave evidence at the Tribunal. Mr O'Shea was asked did he ever give money to the Assistant City Manager, George Redmond. He replied: 'I did. I gave him £200 once and I told him to buy golf balls. Jayz, if you were playing golf with him he'd spend the whole day looking for a ball. If it went into the rough, you'd never finish a game with him.'

Ah, yes. George Redmond. The man whose motto could be 'Show me the money'.

Apart from the £300,000 he had squirrelled away on the Isle of Man, Mr Redmond had nearly £30,000 in spare change in his bathroom. And the Tribunal thought he had several thousand pounds hidden in a 'shed'. But no, it turned out to be 'The Shield' – an insurance company.

George had over twenty different bank accounts and could remember accurately how much he had in each one. ('The Bank of

Ireland, Raheny, had seven pounds in it for over twenty years.') When George declared, 'I'm a heavy saver,' he wasn't joking.

Des O'Neill, Senior Counsel for the Flood Tribunal, asked Mr Redmond about accounts that were opened using fictional names and addresses.

> O'Neill: In respect of the ac-
> counts with financial instit-
> utions such as UDT and Credit
> Finance Bank, you were giving
> fictional addresses; isn't that
> right?
> Redmond: I was giving … well, I
> wasn't giving my home ad-
> dress. I was giving addresses of
> … in the case I gave my … in
> the case of Hollybank; that was
> a good friend of mine. I got his
> consent – I said: 'Can I put it in
> your name?' and he said: 'Yes.'
> O'Neill: Did you then use another
> friend's account in Northbrook
> – sorry: address in Northbrook
> Road. Crosby house was
> another address.
> Redmond: That is, he moved
> from Hollybank, the same
> place. The same man, yes. He is
> deceased by the way. A very
> good friend.
> O'Neill: Did you also indicate at

one point in time that you had an address in Mijas Costa in Spain, in Calahonda?

Redmond: I don't know whether I ever used it … did I use it? I don't know. Maybe I did, yeah. That was a cousin of mine.

O'Neill: Yes. The Credit Finance bank account, which was opened on 20 October 1987, gives your name as Shorsha Mac Raymonn of Villa la Torre, Piesis Bahos, Calle Malaga, Citiode Calahonda, Mijas Costa, Espagna.

Redmond: That was my friend as well. He was a first cousin – not a first cousin – a removed cousin.

O'Neill: The bank account that you opened with Credit Finance in May of 1980 was one in which you had given your address as Oracle Cottage, Alderwinkle, Northants, England.

Redmond: That is true. That was a sister-in-law of mine.

George had so many different addresses when opening bank accounts that the postal service was considering opening a sorting office dedicated to looking after his mail, or at least his brown paper envelopes.

8

# DUNLOP TIRES

Just as the Flood Tribunal looked like it was
getting bogged down with the so-called
Gogarty Module, along came Frank
Dunlop, former Press Secretary for Fianna
Fáil, TV personality and the director of a
highly successful PR firm. Mr Dunlop was
charming, erudite and well capable of
disposing of all questions put to him about
his PR work on behalf of builders and
property developers.

Until the Tribunal accountants discovered a paper trail that lead to an
undisclosed bank account in Rathfarnham.
Mr Justice Flood described it as 'an unusual
bank account. It doesn't have a cheque book;
it is a current account. It has large sums of
money in it and it must have been put to or

designed for a purpose or purposes. There is something unique about it.'

Mr Dunlop was asked to 'reflect on this overnight'. The following morning Mr Hanratty for the Tribunal questioned Mr Dunlop.

> Hanratty: Have you given any thought to the suggestion of the Sole Member yesterday?
>
> Dunlop: Yes, I have, Mr Hanratty.
>
> Hanratty: And having done so, have you anything in addition to tell the Tribunal in connection with this account.
>
> Dunlop: I will answer any question that you ask me, to the best of my ability, in relation to the lodgments and disbursements.

Frank said the account was used to make payments to councillors and officials. The cat was out of the bag, and Mr Dunlop spent a busy few days in the witness box making lists of all those who had benefited from his largesse.

Mr Dunlop clearly looked like a man under severe strain as he answered Mr Hanratty's questions as to who got what, when they got it and how much.

There had been a core of councillors who availed of the 'stash of cash', and during the June elections one member of the 'core' actually asked Mr Dunlop for £40,000.

> Hanratty: When you first met this
> person, was it he who nom-
> inated the figure of £40,000?
> Dunlop: Yes.
> Hanratty: And did he ask you to
> pay him £40,000?
> Dunlop: Yes.
> Hanratty: And when he came to
> your office what ... did you just
> give him the briefcase contain-
> ing the money or did you take it
> out of the briefcase?
> Dunlop: I took it out of the
> briefcase and put it in a bag.
> Hanratty: And was the bag a
> brown paper bag?
> Dunlop: No, it was a plastic bag.

Ah. God be with the days of the free plastic bags. Sure we were all innocent then.

As the years wore on Frank became the Tribunal's resident soprano and each time he entered the witness box he thrilled us with another aria.

Mr Gerard Hogan, Senior Counsel for Denis Mahoney, asked Mr Dunlop about a payment of £2,000 to G.V. Wright. (Mr Wright is a Fianna Fáil politician from the north side of Dublin. A good friend of the Haughey family, he owns a very successful fishmonger business and was in the news last year when he was involved in a drunk-driving accident.)

> Hogan: You have already given evidence to the Tribunal in answer to questions put by Miss Dillon. You described the way in which you secreted the £2,000 in a newspaper.
>
> Dunlop: No, Miss Dillon used the word 'secreted'. I said it was folded into a newspaper.
>
> Hogan: Folded. And just to be clear on this, you took the newspaper and put the money inside the newspaper, is that right?
>
> Dunlop: Have you got a newspaper? You take a newspaper and you put the money in and you fold the newspaper.
>
> Hogan: Yes. And you put it … do you, as it were, open the newspaper, put the money inside … opposite, say, the editorial page, close over the newspaper and then hand it over?
>
> Dunlop: Without any due deference to the media representatives here, let's take a newspaper, let's say *The Irish Times*. Sorry to other people – I am particularly picking *The*

*Irish Times.* You take *The Irish Times*, you put the money in and fold it. You do not open it. You don't put it on the editorial page or the death column, or the sports pages. You fold it into the newspaper.

Hogan: Were you in the habit of doing this?

Dunlop: By that method? No.

Hogan: I think you told Miss Dillon it was the only time you did it?

Dunlop: Yes.

Hogan: Did you use this method instead of the old tried and trusted method?

Dunlop: Which was which?

Hogan: I hope that would speak for itself, Mr Dunlop.

Dunlop: No …

Hogan: The use of either white or brown envelopes?

Dunlop: We are very, very frank. You now use the word brown envelope … I think they are gone out of fashion. I think people now use white envelopes. I have evidence to the effect they do.

Hogan: You may have prompted a fashion change or at least contributed to it?

Dunlop: Some achievement.

The fallout from Mr Dunlop's evidence was that the public now got to hear about Mr Big, Mr Insatiable, Mr 'It's-only-resting-in-my-overseas-bank-account' and even the man who went on the *Late Late Show* to blow his trumpet by saying: 'You try running three houses, three cars, three jobs …' [and three versions of the same story at once] ' … and see how you do.'

Padraig Flynn – or P. Flynn as he likes to be known – really opened a hornet's nest with that remark. The studio audience bristled; the viewers thought it was crass in the extreme. And P. really ruffled the feathers of one Tom Gilmartin, who claims he had given P. a 'donation' of £50,000. Of course P. pocketed the 'donation' for his political expenses; and not a sausage went to Fianna Fáil party headquarters. More cans, more worms.

And of course we also got to hear about a certain Mr Liam Lawlor: the one and only, the man who talked about himself in the third person as if even Liam was in awe of Liam. ('That's not a Liam Lawlor Account. It's a numbered account. If that was a Liam Lawlor account it would have my name on it.')

Liam Lawlor. The hurler on the ditch made good. The man who brought the Tribunal to a halt with his loud lamentation: 'Ah, Holy Mother of Jaysus.'

(At one point during his attendance at

the Mahon Tribunal a reporter asked Liam about Joe Taylor's re-enactments of his evidence on the radio. His reply was, 'Pathetic! Pathetic! That fellow can't do a Dublin accent. Must have a rural background.' Must have known Joe hails from Sligo.)

At the Flood/Mahon Tribunal Liam was constantly taken to task by the Chairman for his interruptions and loud mutterings from the back of the Tribunal chambers. But despite being given the 'red card by the ref', Liam still demanded: 'I am entitled to make a point of order.' John Gallagher S.C. replied: 'Mr Lawlor you are entitled to answer questions here. That's your role. Not to make points of order. This is not the Dáil or anywhere else. Your function is to answer questions to the best of your ability.'

But when Mr Lawlor was asked about the profits he made from his company Irish Consortium, which had dealings overseas, he gave the Tribunal the verbal equivalent of the two fingers, saying, 'It is none of your business and I'm not answering it. If I make profits in the Czech Republic it has nothing to do with this Tribunal, and I don't see the purpose of wasting the time and money of the taxpayer dealing with the Czech Republic.'

Mr Lawlor had a mantra that he repeated over and over to the press – 'I intend to co-operate fully with the Tribunal' – but when he was asked about a payment of £38,000 made by Frank Dunlop to the consultancy firm Long Associates (another of his companies), Mr Lawlor and the Tribunal begged to differ over what was meant by 'co-operating fully'.

And to demonstrate just how 'co-operative' he could be Mr Lawlor went to Mountjoy Jail three times in defiance of a High Court order to co-operate with the Tribunal and furnish documents that the Tribunal lawyers wished to examine.

By an extraordinary coincidence the Tribunal also discovered that a taxi driver named Mr John Long had obtained a credit card for Mr Lawlor's personal use. Mr Gallagher for the Flood Tribunal questioned Mr Long about this.

> Gallagher: Well, do I take it that the credit card was issued to you in your name at 22 Hillcrest Park, Lucan, in or about January of 1999?
>
> Long: Yeah.
>
> Gallagher: Yes, all right. And what did you do with that credit card at that stage, Mr Long?
>
> Long: I gave it to Liam.
>
> Gallagher: Liam who?
>
> Long: Don't be silly now, come on.

Gallagher: Mr Long?

Long: What Liam are we talking about here? There is only one Liam here.

Gallagher: Mr Long, there is a record, there is a record being kept here, it is necessary to be precise.

Long: Sorry. I thought you were being funny again.

Gallagher: What?

Long: Liam Lawlor, there is only one. Whenever I mention 'Liam' it is Liam Lawlor. There is only one Liam Lawlor.

Liam Lawlor was killed in a tragic car crash in Moscow on 22 October 2005. The legend died with him.

### ANOTHER MUSICAL INTERLUDE

You could sing the following to the tune of 'He's in the Jailhouse Now':

Liam was a Dub
Tough as they come.
He'd stand up and fight rather than
    run.
He thought he was way outside the law,
But he didn't heed the warning,
Got three months for his scornin'.
They banged him up inside of
    Mountjoy Jail.

He's in the jailhouse now!
He's in the jailhouse now!
He's in there with the lags
Doin' deals for roll-up fags –
He's in the jailhouse now!

Liam liked to strut and swagger
Like Lucan's toughest blagger,
And pulling strokes was Liam's
    favourite game.
But his brass neck got dented
When the judge said 'less he repented
He'd lock him up an' take away his
    mobile phone.

He's in the jailhouse now!
He's in the jailhouse now!
Well the judge gave him the chop,
Said the rot's just gotta stop –
He's in the jailhouse now!

Liam got out of chokey,
Gave the press the slip by hokey,
Sped off to join his pals in Leinster
    House.
But then Flood he came a callin'
And Liam started bawlin',
Swore he gave them every file he had.
He's in the jailhouse now!
He's in the jailhouse now!
He's no longer Liam Lawlor,
He's just a number to the warder –
He's in the jailhouse now!

# 9

# A Lawlor unto Himself

Jail can do strange things to a man. It can make him hard, cynical and ruthless. But in Liam's case it was much worse. Overnight, Liam Lawlor became 'Liam the Lawyer'.

And just in time. For coming down the line was the man with the billion pound investment for Quarryvale, a large tract of prime west Dublin land, and a development plan for the inner city quays. And the man that seven cabinet ministers of a cash-strapped Government have no recollection of ever meeting – Sligo-born property developer Mr Tom Gilmartin.

Gilmartin told the Mahon Tribunal he had found himself frustrated at every turn: 'I felt it despicable that you came into a country that was on its knees. And there's queues down at the American Embassy and elsewhere, with the kids leaving and walking the streets of London and on the underground begging when they couldn't get a job ... absolutely despicable that the people who run this country have no interest whatsoever in these people, other than feathering their own nest.'

Mr Gilmartin told the Tribunal that, at a meeting with the magnificent seven in Leinster House, he was approached by a mystery man in a tweed jacket who said to him, as Gilmartin told it: "'We think you should give us some of that money up front. We want you to deposit five million pounds and we want it deposited into an Isle of Man account." I turned to him and I told him: "You people make the so and so Mafia look like monks." I said, "You're not serious are you?" and I walked away. He grabbed me by the hand and he says: "You so and so could wind up in the Liffey for that statement." So I told him to so and so off and walked on.'

Tom is too much of a gentleman to use a certain four letter word in the witness box.

As Mr Gilmartin was getting into the lift to leave this meeting he was approached by Sean Walsh, a backbench T.D. Gilmartin later repeated the conversation at the Tribunal:

Gilmartin: 'Remember you're being shafted, you're being set up, you must watch your back.'

John Gallagher S.C.: You said his parting words to you were 'watch yourself, watch Lawlor'.

Gilmartin: Yeah ...

The Chandler-esque drama enacted at Government buildings was described by Bertie Ahern as 'an informal chit-chat gathering in the corridor, shake hands, say "Hello."' What must it be like in the corridors of power when the 'Monks' *really* get serious?

Bertie may have given us a hint about the possible consequences when he told the Tribunal: 'Mary O'Rourke remembered the doors in, but there is only ... if she went out that door she would have fell off the first floor because there is no door.'

Liam the Lawyer was having none of Tom Gilmartin's air of do-goodness and he tore into him like a devil with his first brief, saying: 'We are all out of step except Tom. He left the west of Ireland in proverbial bare feet and trousers in a bad condition. He came back to save the country by driving a coach and four through the '72 County Development Plan. We were to discard the plan to facilitate Mr Gilmartin's greed. Liffey Valley, let's be clear, is built in the wrong place today. It had nothing to do with Mafias or Monks or hundreds of thousands of pounds on demand here there and everywhere. So we can question, cross-examine, query and sit here for days in the coming weeks at enormous time and expense trawling through Mr Gilmartin's pack of lies.'

And so for the two weeks that Liam cross-examined Tom, the pair traded insults like fishwives, each calling the other a liar, a gangster and a crook.

Not to be outdone by the muck-raking of amateur barrister Liam, Mr Conor Maguire, S.C. for Bertie Ahern, indulged in a spot of slurry-spreading himself.

> Maguire: I want to suggest to you that your evidence is less than frank; in other words, that you're shifty and that you have given dishonest evidence.
>
> Gilmartin: No. Sorry, how would I be less than frank? I think I've answered you quite forthright.
>
> Maguire: It's not the first time that you've been described as shifty or in fact not having …
>
> Gilmartin: I was never shifty.
>
> Maguire: Do you remember Judge Sheehy calling you a shifty witness and saying that you had all the hallmarks of a dishonest

witness when you were in court
in Cavan over land?

The public gallery at the Tribunal
booed and jeered this line of questioning. It
seemed that the Taoiseach's legal team had
gone back over a quarter of a century to
5 May 1978 to a report in a local Cavan
paper about a court case involving Mr
Gilmartin and the sale of land.

When Mr Hugh O'Neill, S.C. for Mr
Gilmartin, questioned Mr Bertie Ahern
about this so-called hatchet job on his
client, those who were there described
Bertie's cocker spaniel eyes turning to
gimlets and his mouth becoming a razor
blade slit in a face white with anger.

> O'Neill: Do you recognise Mr
> Gilmartin? He is sitting to my
> left, four seats away, can you
> see him?
> Ahern: I can't.
> O'Neill: That's Mr Gilmartin and
> you recognise him?
> Ahern: I've been looking at him
> in the newspapers every day for
> the past few weeks.
> O'Neill: This is the gentleman
> that you regard as being shifty,
> is that right?
> Ahern: Did I say that?
> O'Neill: Well, do you regard him
> as being shifty?

Ahern: Did I say that?

O'Neill: I'm not saying that you said that but your counsel did.

Ahern: Did I say that?

O'Neill: No, you didn't. Do you regard him as shifty?

Ahern: No, I don't.

O'Neill: Do you regard the evidence he has given insofar as you are aware of it to be dishonest evidence?

Ahern: I think you were quoting from a previous time.

O'Neill: That line of questioning was pursued on your behalf, Mr Ahern. Do you disassociate yourself from it?

Ahern: I did not say and I never said that Mr Gilmartin is shifty or [that he gave] dishonest evidence. He has changed his story many times.

O'Neill: Do you disassociate yourself from those remarks?

Ahern: Well, I didn't say them.

O'Neill: Do you disassociate yourself from those remarks?

Ahern: I didn't say them or wouldn't say that.

O'Neill: How many times do I have to ask then?

Ahern: How many times do I have to answer it, Mr O'Neill?

And maybe because it was Spy Wednesday we all expected a cock to crow for the third time when Bertie made his final denial.

It was the zenith of the Tribunal's activities. The building had been filled to capacity with journalists, members of the public and lawyers who wanted to see the Legal Eagles versus Anorak Man. Rumour had it that at lunch time the so-called Drumcondra Mafia (Bertie's constituency claque) had packed out the front rows of the public gallery with poodles. There was a strong Garda presence and one member of the public was forcibly removed from the building for being too vociferous in his condemnation of Bertie.

The cross-examination started late, but because the Taoiseach had only a short window of opportunity in which to give evidence, the proceedings went on well into the evening.

With so many people packed into the Tribunal chambers body heat (and its associated odour) rose. The event had all the fascination of a show trial. Every word uttered seemed to carry enormous gravitas. Would Bertie stumble? Would the mask slip sufficiently for the Teflon Taoiseach to show spots of tarnish? No. It was a battle of wills and Bertie's will to survive proved the strongest. When the Taoiseach finished giving his evidence he was mobbed by members of the press, photographers and all his panting poodles.

From that day on the Flood/Mahon Tribunal began its slide into obscurity. Ennui and boredom set in with the general public. Those with skeletons yet to be unearthed would like to see the Tribunal put out of its misery with a swift bullet to the head. However, its demise will in all probability be brought about by a drying up of funds. Tribunals as a way of investigating matters of grave concern were first set up by the British in India during the Raj. That alone should have made us suspicious as to the motives of the Government when they decided to investigate political corruption by means of a tribunal.

# 10

# THE TRIBUNAL BALL

For those of you who haven't been there, the Flood/Mahon Tribunal takes place in a large cavernous building that was formerly the old printworks in Dublin Castle. In fact many say it's still used to print money – by lawyers. Anyway, there's a certain irony in the fact that the Tribunal hall is right beside the Revenue Commissioners.

One hot afternoon when tempers were frayed and senior counsel were arguing fiercely over some point of law, a man in a brown leather bomber jacket, checked shirt, cowboy boots and jeans rushed into the Tribunal chambers, holding a piece of paper in his hands and looking distraught. It was like a scene from a movie. We all expected him to hold up the paper and say,

'Here it is! I've found the missing evidence!'

But instead Bomber Jacket looked around at the crowd and sat down next to the journalist Frank Connolly. He stayed there, extremely tense and agitated, for about five minutes. Eventually he turned to Frank Connolly and said, 'What time is it?'

'Ten past four,' Connolly replied.

'Jaysus,' Bomber Jacket said, 'those fuckers in the Revenue Commission told me to be here at four to see about me tax. They'll be fuckin' all day gettin' through this lot before I'm called. Ah, fuck this!'

And with that he stood up, gave a filthy look to the judges' bench and legged it.

'A feisty old curmudgeon' is how the journalist Sam Smyth described James Gogarty, but there was a lot more to him than that. Gogarty had the happy knack of using a few well-chosen words to puncture the great windbag that is the legal system.

One day near the end of his marathon forty days in the witness box, copies of some legal papers were asked for by counsels at the Tribunal. Unfortunately the photocopying machine broke down and there followed one of those tension filled lulls in the proceedings.

People fidgeted in their seats, cleared their throats and felt ill at ease until Gogarty called over one of the law clerks, held out a glass and said, 'Would you ever pour us out a glass of water there, like a good girl?'

The water was poured, Gogarty took a few sips, looked at the glass. All eyes in the Tribunal hall were on him. 'Aaaaah, that's grand, grand and do you know what? It would be even better if you had a drop of whiskey to go with it,' he said.

The public started to laugh and Gogarty took his cue. 'Would anyone like to come up here and sing an oul' bar of a song for us, to liven the place up? Can anyone sing us an oul' song?'

James Gogarty died peacefully on 15 September 2005. Ní bheidh a leithéid ann arís.

## A Final Musical Interlude
You could sing this to the air of 'Flanagan's Ball':

*The Tribunal Ball*
(with apologies to Percy French)

The Flood Tribunal in Dubbelin Castle
Heard Gogarty's evidence, warts and
    all.
How they gave lots of money to
    Raphael Burke
When out to the minister's house they

did call.
'There were two in the car with me,'
 says Gogarty.
'Murphy and Bailey on our trip to see
 Burke.
When I asked would we get a receipt
 for the money
Bailey turns round and says he: "Will
 we fuck!"'

Six long years we spent in Dubbelin,
Six long years in pursuit of the truth.
Six long years listening to witnesses
Swearing their oath on God's Holy Book.

*Chorus*
Redmond flew out and Redmond flew
 back again.
CAB brought him in and CAB let him
 out again.
Flood took them on but CAB fought
 back with him,
By refusing to dance at the Tribunal
 Ball.

Then in July we thought we'd hear
 something
When man of the match, Ray Burke,
 took the stand.
He'd tell us about the brown paper
 parcel
And how he came in for a cool thirty
 grand.

When he got in the box Ray started to
bluster.
The poor man he thought he was back
in the Dáil.
'Mr Chairman, I spent a few grand on
elections,
And the rest's in safe-keeping for
Fianna Fáil.'

Ten long years it's been in his bank
account,
Ten long years it's been salted away.
Ten long years the Fianna Fáil party
Knew nothing about the donation to Ray.

*Chorus*
Ray stepped in and Ray stepped out
again.
Ray grew thin and Ray grew stout
again.
Ray should thank his lawyer Joe
Finnegan,
Who taught him to dance for the
Tribunal Ball.

If you're looking for lawyers go down to
the castle;
You'll see the bigwigs all milling
around.
The best of the bar perform there daily
And worth every penny of 32 million
pound.

There's Cooney and Cush – not
    forgetting Dan Herbert –
There's Alan, Leahy and yer man from
    Smith Foy,
O'Moore and Callanan with Gerry
    Sheedy,
And Anthony Harris in Redmond's
    employ.

*Chorus*
Fourteen hundred for each Senior
    Counsel,
Sixty grand for the doctors of spin.
Thirty two million quid and steadily
    risin'
But who gives a damn when the lawyers
    all win.

O'Neill stepped out and Gallagher
    stepped in again,
Dillon stepped in, Hanratty stepped out
    again.
Flood had to hear the whole shaggin'
    lot of them
Taking the floor at the Tribunal Ball.

# AFTERWORD

## BY VINCENT BROWNE

The torrent of controversy surrounding
the death of Liam Lawlor in Moscow was
inevitable. The raging personality who
dominated the hearings of the Planning
Tribunal for years could hardly exit life
quietly. His furious bombasts were brought
to listeners so vividly and hilariously by Joe
Taylor on the *Tonight* programme on
R.T.É. Radio One. Liam Lawlor defied
Tribunal-fatigue. It will be more difficult to
defy that now he is gone.

Another personality who dominated
the early days/months/years of the Planning Tribunal, James Gogarty, has also
passed on. Joe Taylor memorably brought
James Gogarty to *Tonight* listeners. That

famous purported exchange between Gogarty and Michael Bailey as they were on their way to see Ray Burke in June 1989 has entered the lexicon of political folklore, although very likely an invention of James Gogarty, as indeed, very probably, was a lot of the rest of his evidence.

As we go to press, there is a concerted publicity campaign, stoked by well-paid P.R. consultants, to bring the Tribunal process to an end. The contention advanced is that Tribunals have cost a fortune and are getting nowhere, that they have abused the rights and reputations of citizens and that they will continue endlessly unless halted now.

There is certainly evidence that Tribunals have abused their powers, as the case taken by Owen O'Callaghan against the Planning Tribunal has established. There is also reason to be sceptical about some of the findings of Feargus Flood in the celebrated second interim report issued by him in September 2002. But the Tribunals have uncovered a scale of corruption at local government level involving politicians and officials that is truly startling. They have also revealed professionally organised tax scams involving many of the most reputed names in Irish business. As a consequence of the latter hundreds of millions of euros have been recovered in taxes, interest and penalties. The Tribunals have also disclosed the murky interface between business and politics.

The Moriarty Tribunal has been censured for its persistence with its inquiries into the award of the second mobile phone license to the company headed by Denis O'Brien. It is argued that there is no evidence that the process or the project team that recommended on the award of the license was contaminated and therefore that the enquires into whether Denis O'Brien gave monies to the minister concerned, Michael Lowry, are irrelevant. In a robust response to these representations Mr Justice Michael Moriarty has pointed out that there is evidence that at least raises questions about the integrity of the process. The award of the second mobile phone license was, by far, the greatest benefit ever awarded a company in Ireland. If it is found that this was done corruptly it will be a major indictment of our system of government as well as, of course, of Fine Gael, the then lead party in government and the party of which Michael Lowry was a member. It is of paramount importance that the investigation of this issue proceed.

The most odious conduct to be revealed by any of the Tribunals was, in my view, on the part of Frank Dunlop. As is characteristic of him he has tried to deflect blame by insisting the system was corrupt before he got there and he merely played the games in accordance with the prevailing rules. He has insisted that all the councillors and officials he bribed came to him in the first instance seeking bribes. Even if this contention were true how would they have known that he was a likely touch, that they could go to him in confidence and, in effect, disclose their corrupt intentions, knowing he would not blow the whistle on him? And what is most odious now is that he, having corrupted them, takes credit for exposing them.

Frank Dunlop was no mere party functionary. He was embedded in Jack Lynch's Fianna Fáil, part of the set that included George Colley, Des O'Malley, Mary Harney and Martin O'Donoghue. The very people who have insisted that the font and origin of all corruption in Irish politics lay in their party adversary, Charles Haughey. Joe Taylor magnificently caught the preciousness, the assumed grandeur, the acquired polished accent of Frank Dunlop, and the denial.

Tribunals are likely to remain a feature of Irish politics because of the incapacity of other investigative agencies to unravel the truth about corruption. The media has neither the ability nor the will to uncover evidence of corruption. In part because the media itself is so compromised – Independent Newspapers, the dominant force in Irish media, is controlled by a person, Tony O'Reilly, whose business tentacles extend right into the heart of politics (see below). In part because the media does not have the powers of 'compellability' (the capacity to compel witnesses and documents) which Tribunals enjoy.

Neither can the Oireachtas exercise investigative powers. The Supreme Court has so ordained and, anyway, Oireachtas committees of inquiry are so hamstrung by party whips and political agendas that they are unable to operate as reliable independent investigative agencies.

So we are left with Tribunals, expensive and protracted. But how else are we to exercise surveillance on the conduct of public affairs?

There is so much, however, that remains unexamined. For instance, how was it that the *Irish Press* group, founded and financed by public subscriptions from people anxious to establish an alternative media voice in Ireland in the late 1920s, became the plaything and property of the de Valera family? Or more recently, how was it that the consortium headed by Tony O'Reilly, Valentia, was facilitated by a private undertaking to change the tax laws in relation to worker shareholdings to enable it to take over Eircom? Even when it was known that the Valentia bid would necessarily involve the degradation of the country's telecommunications infrastructure because of the way the Valentia take-over was to be financed.

So with a bit of luck Joe Taylor and Malcolm Douglas have long and lucrative careers ahead as interpreters of Tribunals, provided of course that sanity does not intervene and the live and recorded broadcasting of Tribunal proceedings is permitted.

October 2005

# BiTS foR ANoRaKS i

## Statement by An Taoiseach Bertie Ahern on the McCracken Tribunal Report

'I would like to congratulate Mr Justice McCracken and his Tribunal on their excellent work and report on the Dunne's payments to politicians.

'Our duty is to guard our country and our democratic system from any taint or suspicion of corruption, and to remove any obvious or possible source of danger. While in the terms of the Tribunal's Report 'no political impropriety' has been shown to have occurred, the acceptance of large gifts or payments or personal benefits in a surreptitious manner or the large scale evasion of tax and exchange control regulations by even one or two senior serving politicians or members of Government is deeply damaging to trust in politics and a serious breach of it, and every effort must be made that is humanly possible to ensure that it cannot happen again.

'Honesty and truthfulness and integrity are fundamental requirements of those who serve in public life and who hold positions of great trust. All of us are deeply dismayed at the way in which in certain instances investigated by the Tribunal there has been a falling so far short of these ideals in an indefensible and disgraceful manner.

'The Government welcomes and will study further the recommendations of the Report, with a view to their full and speedy implementation. It may indeed be necessary in certain instances to go beyond them.

'Our concern is to establish firm and workable rules for the governance of our democracy that will be fully observed in letter and in spirit. Many of the necessary mechanisms are already in place under the Ethics in Public Office Act, and the Electoral Act. But it is clear that these will now need to be reviewed, and further improved. This we will do urgently.

'Without prejudice to the need for any immediate further investigations relating to matters raised by the Tribunal Report – and this week the Government at its meeting on Thursday will be considering the necessity of a second Tribunal – we will be looking to establish expeditiously by legislation a permanent body, such as a Public Ethics commission, that will be capable of investigating with the assistance of all the resources of the State any accusations of public impropriety that appear to have any substance prima facie. I am determined to protect the integrity of our political decision-making and to see that any taint to that integrity is exposed. I intend to consult and work with other party leaders to ensure that the mechanisms we establish have maximum efficacy. The Attorney General has already begun to work on the necessary legislation, which we would hope to have in force by the end of October. The Commission would in principle have the power to carry out any further investigation required into any serious matter brought to its attention.

'It is the view of the Government that the investigation of the Ansbacher accounts should be further pursued by the Tribunal. The Government also expects the relevant agencies of the State to take all necessary action on foot of this Report.

'There are many other aspects and implications of the Report that will require more detailed consideration and debate, both by the Government and the Dáil. But in all decisions that we take the good name of Ireland and the protection of our democracy will be paramount.

'Our State is much more prosperous today than when it was established. But in terms of integrity we should adhere to the simple and straightforward ideals of our founders. We owe it to the least fortunate of our citizens to ensure that public decisions affecting everyone's welfare are taken only on grounds of equity and the public good, and to ensure that possession of wealth can never purchase privately political favours.'

25 August 1997

# BiTS fOR ANOraKS ii

## TiMELiNE Of EVENTS CONCERNiNg DUNNES STORES, CHarLES HauGHEY aND THE REVENUE COMMiSSiONERS

**January–February 1987:** bearer cheques amounting to £32,200 from Ben Dunne lodged in an account in Guinness and Mahon for the benefit of former Fianna Fáil leader Charles Haughey.

**10 March 1987:** change of government; Haughey elected Taoiseach.

**16 March 1987:** assessment of discretionary trust tax raised by the Revenue

Commissioners appealed by Dunnes Trustees to the Appeal Commissioners and settled. Liability not discharged by Dunnes until 25 May 1987.

**Prior to May 1987, possibly in February/March:** Noel Fox acts as conduit for communications between Des Traynor and Ben Dunne in connection with financial assistance for Haughey. Dunne says he will take responsibility for the full amount needed, estimated at £1 million.

**Prior to 5 May 1987, possibly on April 27:** Haughey 'appears to have intervened in the dealings between the Dunnes Trustees and the Revenue', and asked Seamus Parceir, the Revenue chairman, to meet Dunne.

**5 May 1987:** Parceir says he met Dunne to discuss the settlement of a capital gains tax assessment of £38.8 million. Parceir subsequently holds meetings with officials to discuss this.

**20 May 1987:** Matt Price of Dunnes Stores (Bangor), at the request of Fox and Dunne, draws a cheque for £282,500 sterling in favour of Triple-plan. Fox subsequently gives the cheque to Traynor.

**25 May 1987** Fox discharges the liabilities of the Dunnes Trustees to the Revenue. Parceir agrees with Fox that the continuing interest that the Dunnes Trustees had agreed to pay under the terms of the settlement, amounting to £62,450, need not be paid.

**4 June 1987**: Parceir informs Dunne and Fox that the Revenue would agree a compromise on the £38.8 million assessment for capital gains tax at a figure of £16 million. Parceir meets Dunne and Fox on at least two subsequent occasions. The final meeting is on 10 or 11 September 1987. Parceir retires on September 11.

**28 February 1988**: Appeals Commissioner lists Dunnes appeal against the capital gains tax assessment by Revenue for hearing.

**1 March 1988**: Haughey directs the new Revenue chairman, Philip Curran, to talk to him about Dunne. The two meet on 11 March and Haughey tells Curran he will get Dunne to contact him.

**21 March 1988**: Curran meets Dunne.

**22/23 September 1988**: capital gains tax appeal decided in favour of Dunnes Trustees.

# Bits for Anoraks iii

## Events Leading to the Setting up of the Flood Tribunal

**On 3 July 1995** a notice appeared in two Irish daily papers offering a reward of £10,000 to anyone with information that would lead to the conviction of persons involved in corruption in the planning process. Donnelly Neary Donnelly Solicitors in Newry, Co. Down, placed this notice on behalf of unnamed clients.

**On 31 March 1996** the journalist Frank Connolly wrote an article in the *Sunday Business Post* claiming that a person had contacted the Newry solicitors to say that he had personally paid a politician

£40,000 in return for a promise to have 1,000 acres of land re-zoned for housing. The headline in the paper ran ' Fianna Fáil Politician Paid off by Developer'.

**On 7 April 1996** Frank Connolly again wrote in the *Sunday Business Post* that on top of the £40,000 paid by the company director to the politician, a further £40,000 was paid by a property developer to the same politician just days before the General Election in 1989.

**On 20 July 1997** Matt Cooper, writing in the *Sunday Tribune*, named Mr Ray Burke as the politician who had received the money from a property company called Bovale Developments. The brothers Tom and Michael (Mick) Bailey were executive directors of Bovale.

**On 10 August 1997** the *Sunday Business Post* published an article by Frank Connolly stating that a Mr James Gogarty, an excutive of Joseph Murphy Structural Engineers (J.M.S.E.), had told him that two envelopes had been handed over to Ray Burke. One containing £40,000 from J.M.S.E. and the other envelope which Gogarty presumed matched this amount (i.e. contained £40,000) was donated by Mick Bailey on behalf of Bovale Developments.

**On 7 August 1997** Mr Ray Burke T.D., Minister for Foreign Affairs, issued a public statement berating the vicious campaign of rumour and innuendo that had been set up to smear and tarnish his image. He found himself the victim of a campaign of calumny and abuse. He found the matter totally unacceptable and stated that if any further untruths were published about him he would take all the necessary steps to vindicate his good name and reputation.

**On 10 September 1997** Mr Burke made a statement in Dáil Éireann in which he told the House, 'I have done nothing illegal, unethical or improper.' Mr Burke then said 'Mr Gogarty's allegations against me form merely a small part of the allegations being thrown by him against his former employers from whom he parted in acrimonious circumstances.' Mr Burke closed his address to the House by saying, 'There may be a bit of blood lust today for my neck, but we are setting a precedent that we will all regret in future. I have no intention of subjecting myself to a show trial to satisify anyone's political agenda.'

When asked by Mr Jim O'Keefe if he had lodged any monies in overseas bank accounts Mr Burke bristled with indignation and replied: 'I have bared my soul to the House today and I find the Deputy's question offensive in the extreme at this stage. I have no overseas bank account.'

Mr Burke must have completely forgotten about his Caviar Bank account in the Isle of Man – making that the first of his many memory lapses in relation to his financial affairs.

**On 1 October 1997** An Taoiseach Mr Bertie Ahern (having been up every tree in North County Dublin looking for 'evidence' of Ray Burke's shenanigans) informed the Oireachteas that he was establishing a Tribunal to investigate matters relating to land development. Six days later Mr Burke resigned his seat as a Member of Dáil Éireann.